A CASE STUDINSANITY DEFENSE

THE TRIAL OF JOHN W. HINCKLEY, JR.

SECOND EDITION

By

RICHARD J. BONNIE
John S. Battle Professor of Law
Roy L. and Rosamond Woodruff Morgan Research
Professor of Law
Director, Institute of Law, Psychiatry & Public Policy
University of Virginia

JOHN C. JEFFRIES, JR.
Emerson Spies Professor of Law
William L. Matheson & Robert M. Morgenthau
Distinguished Professor of Law
University of Virginia

PETER W. LOW
Vice President and Provost of the University
Hardy Cross Dillard Professor of Law
University of Virginia

New York, New York
FOUNDATION PRESS
2000

Cover by Cathryn E. Low, Low Co.com

TEXT IS PRINTED ON 10% POST
CONSUMER RECYCLED PAPER

TABLE OF CONTENTS

PART IV THE AFTERMATH

*

A CASE STUDY IN THE INSANITY DEFENSE

THE TRIAL OF JOHN W. HINCKLEY, JR.

*

INTRODUCTION

On March 30, 1981, John W. Hinckley, Jr., shot and wounded President Ronald Reagan as the President was walking to his limousine after an appearance at the Hilton Hotel in Washington, D.C. Three other people were hit by Hinckley's shots. One of them—Press Secretary James Brady—was gravely injured by a wound in the head. The shooting was observed by scores of eyewitnesses and seen by millions of others on television. Hinckley was immediately apprehended by federal law enforcement officials.

Hinckley was charged with 13 crimes. His trial began on May 4, 1982, and lasted seven weeks. The transcript of the trial extends to 7,342 pages, most of which are devoted to testimony on Hinckley's primary defense: that at the time of his conduct he was legally insane. On June 21, after deliberating for three days, the jury returned a verdict of not guilty by reason of insanity. This verdict extended to each of the 13 crimes Hinckley was accused of committing. Hinckley was thereafter committed to St. Elizabeth's Hospital, where he still resides.

These events captured the attention of the nation. The general reaction to Hinckley's acquittal was outrage and disbelief. Many people could not understand how Hinckley could be found "not guilty"—and could escape punishment—for a planned assassination attempt resulting in serious injury to four people. This issue was fully ventilated in the press and remains the subject of continuing debate.

There was also widespread reaction in the legislatures of the country. How the insanity defense should be formulated has always been a difficult and controversial issue. The adverse reaction to the Hinckley acquittal brought forth new calls to restrict the scope of the defense. As a result, significant changes in the insanity defense have been enacted by the Congress and by half of the states.

In many respects, the *Hinckley* case presents in microcosm most of the difficult issues involved in the effort to formulate an appropriate insanity defense. This book examines these issues through consideration of the actual testimony in the case.

First, however, it is necessary to provide some background on the nature of the problem and on the history of the insanity defense. This is done in Part I below. Part II then presents the *Hinckley* case itself, primarily through excerpts from the actual trial testimony, from the arguments of counsel, and from the judge's instructions to the jury. Part III raises for consideration and study some of the difficult questions of

1

policy presented by the *Hinckley* trial and examines the reforms of the law of insanity recently adopted by various legislatures around the country. Finally, Part IV considers the hospitalization and treatment of Hinckley since his insanity acquittal and raises general issues concerning the commitment and release of persons acquitted by reason of insanity.

———

PART I

BACKGROUND

INTRODUCTION TO THE INSANITY DEFENSE

1. Context. The insanity defense is a difficult subject. Indeed, few aspects of the criminal law have been more controversial over the years. Although insanity has been a defense to a charge of crime for centuries, contemporary critics continue to debate the types of mental incapacity that should excuse criminal behavior, and even whether there should be an insanity defense at all. The dimensions of this dispute can readily be seen in any representative sample of professional commentary on the subject.[a] Proposals to broaden the defense compete with calls for its abolition. Many argue for limitations on the scope of the defense. That there is little agreement among the experts makes the problem even harder for the lay person to understand.

There are at least three dimensions of the controversy. First, specialists in the field of criminal law cannot reach a consensus on whether an insanity defense is consistent with the purposes of the criminal law, and if so, how it can best be formulated in order to serve those purposes. Second, specialists in the mental health disciplines bring varying perspectives to bear on the relationship between mental disorder and criminal behavior. Third, those who work in the field of criminal law and those who work in the field of mental health have difficulty communicating with each other. Perhaps the most important reason for this difficulty is that the two disciplines have different, and sometimes incompatible, objectives.

2. The Criminal Law. Proponents of an insanity defense begin with the assertion that the criminal law has (and must have) a basis in common morality. In this view, criminal punishment is inappropriate unless the defendant can be "blamed" for the offense: to say that a person is "guilty" of murder or theft or rape is a public expression of moral disapproval, an official "scarlet letter." Moreover, the proponents continue, moral disapproval of conduct is based on certain premises about the capacities of people to make autonomous choices over their behavior. It is inappropriate, for example, morally to condemn a child for

[a] For example, see Abraham Goldstein, The Insanity Defense (1967); Joel Feinberg, Doing and Deserving: Essays in the Theory of Responsibility (1970); Herbert Fingarette and Ann F. Hasse, Mental Disabilities and Criminal Responsibility (1979); Norval Morris, Madness and the Criminal Law (1982); Donald H.J. Hermann, The Insanity Defense: Philosophical, Historical and Legal Perspectives (1983); Michael Moore, Law and Psychiatry: Rethinking the Relationship (1984); Michael Perlin, The Jurisprudence of the Insanity Defense (1994).

3

behavior she or he is not old enough to understand. We do not convict small children of crimes for this reason. It follows, say the proponents of an insanity defense, that since mental illness can profoundly affect one's cognitive and emotional functioning, a defense must be afforded in cases where, due to mental illness, the defendant is unable to exercise "normal" capacities for rational choice.

Part of the difficulty with this position is that an insanity defense is necessarily of vague and indeterminate scope. It is hard to describe with any precision what it means to say that a person is or is not able to exercise "normal" choices about how to behave, and accordingly hard to measure when a person ought or ought not to be held criminally responsible for wrongful behavior. We can all agree that a person so insane as to mistake strangling a spouse for squeezing lemons should not be judged "guilty" of a criminal offense. But such cases rarely arise. The cases that more often arise involve people who are not so insane as that. They present, as did the trial of John Hinckley, much closer questions about the meaning of moral "guilt" and the proper scope of an insanity defense.

The problem is compounded when other purposes of the criminal law are considered. The criminal law has, to be sure, a strong moral underpinning, focusing on whether a person can justly be "blamed" for criminal behavior. But the criminal law has other goals as well, most prominently goals of prevention and public protection. The criminal process is designed not merely to punish persons who have committed a crime but also to deter potential criminals and to incapacitate those who pose a danger to the public. The insanity defense may well be thought to compromise these goals.

Consider first the goal of deterrence. The deterrence of potential criminals depends on public perception of a credible threat of conviction and punishment for those who would commit a crime. This goal would be undermined by providing a defense of vague and indeterminate scope that is inconsistently applied and that can be, and sometimes has been, faked. It would also be undermined if the message of the successful assertion of an insanity defense—as was widely perceived in the *Hinckley* case—is that the defendant "got away with it" by being acquitted.

Now consider the goal of incapacitating those who pose a danger to the public. This goal would be undermined if the law failed to provide a mechanism for confining dangerous persons who had been acquitted by reason of insanity. Of course, public protection from these people can to some extent be accomplished by the civil commitment of the mentally ill or, as happened in Hinckley's case, by commitment after an acquittal by reason of insanity. But whether the goal of incapacitation is served by such confinement may depend on how easy it is for someone to be released and how accurately it can be determined that the person is no longer dangerous.

The usual criteria for release of a person who has been committed after an insanity acquittal include whether the person poses a present danger to the public. Leaving aside the difficulty of predicting such dangerousness with any accuracy, release of a person who is no longer "dangerous" still can undermine the punitive and deterrent functions of the criminal law. Consider, for example, the likely public reaction if Hinckley had been released from St. Elizabeth's one or two years after his acquittal. Even if the doctors were right that Hinckley no longer presented a public danger, and even if their prediction was borne out by subsequent events, it is by no means clear that everyone would agree that the proper goals of the criminal law would have been satisfied.

3. Integrating Mental Health Knowledge with the Criminal Law. Accommodating the various objectives of the criminal law is difficult enough standing alone. The problem is further complicated when the views and perspectives of specialists in the field of mental health are taken into account.

The difficulties begin with the fact that the insanity defense rests on an uncertain scientific foundation. Simply stated, the causal factors linking body, mind, and behavior are still poorly understood. The problem is compounded by the fact that many of the operating assumptions of psychiatrists, psychologists, and other professionals who study and treat mental and emotional problems are not subject to empirical assessment or validation.

Moreover, the prevailing clinical understanding of mental health issues is not easily translated into conclusions that can be of use in a legal setting. The reason is that clinical and legal inquiries into the workings of the human mind have vastly different objectives. Clinical study of the human psyche is largely a therapeutic discipline. It is concerned with diagnosis and cure, with how to help those who suffer from mental illness or emotional distress. The criminal law, on the other hand, is focused in large part on blame and responsibility, issues that lie beyond the objectives and expertise of psychiatry, psychology, and related disciplines. To put the point more crudely, professionals who study the human mind do not do so in order to understand the issues of moral accountability with which the criminal law must come to grips. They are not ordinarily concerned with whether a person is too sick to be bad.

The problem is compounded even further by the diversity of perspectives from which the mental health disciplines view the study and treatment of mental, emotional, and behavioral problems. Three perspectives will be described below, although it is important to understand that these approaches are not necessarily mutually exclusive. A given mental health professional will not always use a single perspective in dealing with her or his patients. Instead, many experts believe that a complete understanding of their field requires incorporation of all three perspectives.

(i) The Concept of "Disease." Perhaps the easiest perspective for a lay person to understand draws on traditional medical concepts of "disease" to describe and explain abnormal mental phenomena. This view rests on the assumption that there are categorical differences, with probable biological underpinnings, between individuals who have and those who do not have a mental "disease."

Although most mental health specialists believe that this is an accurate description of some conditions,[b] there is considerable disagreement about the range of conditions for which this perspective is useful. The experts are not of one mind, for example, about whether it is sensible to think of "compulsive" behavior, such as gambling or alcohol abuse, as a "disease." Wherever various experts would draw the lines, in any event, it is clear that viewing mental disorders as a "disease" provides an insufficient framework for the professional to understand and treat all types of psychological and behavioral problems.

(ii) The Concept of "Dimensions." From a second perspective, mental health professionals view individuals as varying from one another along a number of different dimensions, usually characterized as personality traits or behavioral propensities. Just as people are taller or shorter in stature, or brighter or duller in intelligence, so too they tend to be optimistic or pessimistic, psychologically dependent or independent, suspicious or trusting. These characteristics are thought to make individuals more or less likely to respond to events or circumstances in their lives in particular ways (for example, by getting angry, depressed, anxious, or frightened).

When viewed in this way, individual differences are regarded as quantitative rather than qualitative. Thus, the concept of mental disease in the sense of something that one "has" or "does not have" is not pertinent to the concept of personality dimensions. Instead, the focus is on describing and measuring differences in degree. Psychological tests and clinical criteria seeking to measure personality traits or behavioral tendencies place all individuals along a continuum, just as intelligence testing does. Of course, designating the point on the continuum at which the trait should be characterized as "abnormal" (and at which the person should be characterized as "retarded," "dependent," or "paranoid") is necessarily somewhat arbitrary. People can be described as "more" or "less" intelligent, "more" or "less" emotionally dependent on others, or "more" or "less" suspicious of others, but it is not possible to say that a particular individual is *categorically* different from other people.

It is this latter point that poses special difficulties for courts and lawyers. In an important sense the criminal law is faced with an

[b] A good example is manic-depressive illness, which in the current nomenclature is called "bipolar affective disorder."

either/or choice. Questions of degree can be taken into account in determining the seriousness of an offense and in sentencing, but determining whether to impose criminal liability in the first instance presents a categorical choice: the defendant is either guilty or not guilty. And momentous consequences—both for the individual and the public—turn on which determination is made.

(iii) **The Concept of "Psychological Explanation."** The effort of legal institutions to shape and administer an insanity defense is further befuddled by another perspective employed in the study and treatment of mental and emotional problems by many mental health experts. From this third perspective, the expert seeks to identify the conscious and unconscious motivations that lead a given individual to engage in particular behavior. Psychological explanations of this sort have been derived from a variety of theoretical premises, including those developed by Sigmund Freud and Carl Jung. Many of these theories are premised on an essentially deterministic view that people are not always aware of, or in control of, the determinants of their own behavior.

The postulation of psychological explanations for individual behavior poses an additional dilemma for the law. In any given case, mental health professionals could explain the forces that led an offender to behave the way she or he did (for example, the defendant raped the victim "because" he was acting out a deep feeling of self-hatred generated as a result of combat experiences in Vietnam). Yet not every clinical "explanation" of the motivations underlying human behavior should lead to acquittal of a charge of crime. If it did, the law would be required to find virtually all offenders not guilty. The normal operation of the criminal law would be completely swallowed up by the effort to probe the psychological determinants of human behavior. Instead, the insanity defense must draw a line between "explanations" that count and "explanations" that do not count, between explanations that justify a verdict of not guilty by reason of insanity and explanations that merely show why the defendant committed the crime.

To put the point another way, mental health professionals can find psychological explanations for any criminal behavior. The job of the insanity defense is to isolate those few individuals whose mental condition is so grossly abnormal that they can be (and should be) distinguished from the "ordinary" murderers, thieves, and rapists for whom punishment as a criminal is the appropriate sanction. This is an imposing task.

4. **Conclusion.** Despite these difficulties, the criminal law traditionally has recognized a special defense of insanity. From the earliest times, the courts and legislatures have provided for "tests" of criminal responsibility that, if satisfied, would result in an acquittal of crime. The following discussion introduces the major "tests" of responsibility as they have been developed over the years by the courts and legislatures.

HISTORY OF THE INSANITY DEFENSE

1. Early History. Before the 12th century, mental disease apparently had no legal significance in the criminal law.[a] At this time, however, issues of moral fault played little role in any aspect of the criminal law. As the criminal law began to develop notions of moral blame in other areas, "madness" came to be recognized as an excuse for crime. At first insanity was not a bar to conviction, but only a ground for granting a royal pardon. While the records are fragmentary, it appears that the king would order some form of indefinite custody in lieu of execution for those afflicted with "madness." The first recorded case of outright acquittal by reason of insanity occurred in 1505.[b]

The earliest commentator to give sustained attention to the subject was Lord Hale, whose treatise was published posthumously in 1736. According to Hale:[c]

> Man is naturally endowed with these two great faculties, understanding and liberty of will. . . . The consent of the will is that which renders human actions either commendable or culpable. . . . And because the liberty or choice of the will presupposeth an act of understanding to know the thing or action chosen by the will, it follows that, where there is a total defect of the understanding, there is no free act of the will.

Hale distinguished between "total defect of understanding" due to insanity and partial madness involving those who "discover their defect in excessive fears and griefs and yet are not wholly destitute of the use of reason." Conceding that "it is very difficult to define the indivisible line that divides perfect and partial insanity," Hale sought to identify that level of "understanding" necessary for criminal liability by assimilating insanity to infancy: "Such a person as labouring under melancholy distempers hath yet ordinarily as great understanding, as ordinarily a child of 14 years hath, is such a person as may be guilty of . . . felony."

Hale's approach failed to take hold.[d] Instead, as one authority noted, 18th century courts "hark[ed] back strongly to the old ethical basis of criminal responsibility and [made] the test one of capacity to intend evil.

---

[a] For general background on the early history of the insanity defense, see Nigel Walker, Crime and Insanity in England (1968); Homer Crotty, The History of Insanity as a Defense to Crime in English Criminal Law, 12 Calif.L.Rev. 105 (1924); Anthony Platt and Bernard Diamond, The Origins of the "Right and Wrong" Test of Criminal Responsibility and Its Subsequent Development in the United States: An Historical Survey, 54 Calif.L. Rev. 1227 (1966).

[b] Nigel Walker, Crime and Insanity in England 26 (1968). Apparently the offender was set free.

[c] Matthew Hale, The History of Pleas of the Crown 14–15 (Philadelphia 1847) (1st ed. 1736).

[d] Sir James Stephen criticized Hale's comparison of infancy and insanity: "The one is healthy immaturity; the other diseased maturity and between these there is no sort of resemblance." 2 A History of the Criminal Law of England 150–51 (1883).

Could the defendant at the time of the offense 'distinguish good from evil?' "[e] An often-cited example is Justice Tracy's charge to the jury in Arnold's Case, 16 How.St.Tr. 695, 764 (1724), which involved a known madman who killed a nobleman in the delusion that the victim had "bewitched him" and was "the occasion of all the troubles in the nation." After summarizing the evidence, Justice Tracy said that the only question was "whether this man had the use of his reason and senses." He continued:

> [I]t is not every kind of frantic humour or something unaccountable in a man's actions, that points him out to be such a madman as is to be exempted from punishment; it must be a man that is totally deprived of his understanding and memory, and doth not know what he is doing, no more than an infant, than a brute, or a wild beast, such a one is never the object of punishment; therefore I must leave it to your consideration, whether the condition this man was in ... doth shew a man, who knew what he was doing, and was able to distinguish whether he was doing good or evil, and understood what he did. . . .

As late as 1840, no appellate court in England or the United States had settled the law on the defense of insanity. However, the subject received a great deal of attention on both sides of the Atlantic during the middle third of the century. One important development was the publication in 1838 of Isaac Ray's treatise on the Medical Jurisprudence of Insanity, signifying the first efforts of the infant science of psychiatry to influence the development of the law. Another major development was the trial, in 1843, of Daniel M'Naghten.

2. M'Naghten's Case. Modern formulations of the insanity defense derive from the "rules" stated by the House of Lords in Daniel M'Naghten's Case, 10 Cl. & F. 200, 8 Eng.Rep. 718 (H.L.1843).[f] M'Naghten was charged with shooting Edward Drummond, who was secretary to Robert Peel, then the Prime Minister of England. M'Naghten admitted that he had come to London for the purpose of shooting Peel. However, he mistook Drummond for Peel, and shot Drummond by mistake. M'Naghten described his motive as follows:

> The tories in my native city have compelled me to do this. They follow and persecute me wherever I go, and have entirely

[e] Francis Bowes Sayre, Mens Rea, 45 Harv.L.Rev. 974, 1006 (1932).

[f] The history of the M'Naghten case is reviewed, and the relevant documents collected, in Donald West and Andrew Walk, Daniel McNaughton: His Trial and the Aftermath (1977), and in Richard Moran, Knowing Right From Wrong (1981).

M'Naghten's name has been spelled at least 12 different ways. Apparently the traditional spelling—the one used here—is only one that cannot be reconciled with the defendant's own signature. See Bernard Diamond, On the Spelling of Daniel M'Naghten's Name, 25 Ohio St.L.J. 84 (1964). According to Moran, the correct spelling is probably "McNaughtan."

destroyed my peace of mind.... I cannot sleep at night in consequence of the course they pursue towards me.... They have accused me of crimes of which I am not guilty; they do everything in their power to harass and persecute me; in fact they wish to murder me.

The thrust of the medical testimony was that M'Naghten was suffering from what would today be described as delusions of persecution symptomatic of paranoid schizophrenia. One of the medical witnesses concluded that:

The act with which he is charged, coupled with the history of his past life, leaves not the remotest doubt on my mind of the presence of insanity sufficient to deprive the prisoner of all self-control. I consider the act of the prisoner in killing Mr. Drummond to have been committed whilst under a delusion; the act itself I look upon as the crowning act of the whole matter—as the climax—as a carrying out of the pre-existing idea which had haunted him for years.

The expert testimony was summarized in the official reports as follows:

That persons of otherwise sound mind, might be affected by morbid delusions; that the prisoner was in that condition; that a person so labouring under a morbid delusion might have a moral perception of right and wrong, but that in the case of the prisoner it was a delusion which carried him away beyond the power of his own control, and left him no such perception; and that he was not capable of exercising any control over acts which had connexion with his delusion; that it was of the nature of the disease with which the prisoner was affected, to go on gradually until it had reached a climax, when it burst forth with irresistible intensity; that a man might go on for years quietly, though at the same time under its influence, but would all at once break out into the most extravagant and violent paroxysms.

In his charge to the jury, Chief Justice Tindal practically told the jury to find the defendant not guilty by reason of insanity. He observed "that the whole of the medical evidence is on one side and that there is no part of it which leaves any doubt on the mind." He then instructed the jury that the verdict should turn on the answer to the following question:

[W]hether ... at the time the act was committed [M'Naghten] had that competent use of his understanding as that he knew that he was doing, by the very act itself, a wicked and a wrong thing. If he was not sensible at the time he committed that act, that it was a violation of the law of God or of man, undoubtedly he was not responsible for that act, or liable to any punishment whatever flowing from that act.... But if ... you think the prisoner capable of distinguishing between right and wrong, then he was a responsible agent. . . .

The jury returned a verdict of not guilty by reason of insanity.[g] This verdict caused considerable popular alarm and was regarded with particular concern by Queen Victoria.[h] As a result, the House of Lords asked the judges of that body to give an advisory opinion regarding the answers to five questions "on the law governing such cases." The combined answers to two of those questions have come to be known as the *M'Naghten* rules:

> [E]very man is to be presumed to be sane. . . . [T]o establish a defence on the ground of insanity, it must be clearly proved that, at the time of the committing of the act, the party accused was <u>labouring under such a defect of reason</u>, from disease of the mind, as not to know the nature and quality of the act he was doing; <u>or</u> if he did know it, that he did not know he was doing what was wrong. *notunderstand*

Notice three features of this formulation:

> First, it is predicated on proof that the defendant was suffering from "a defect of reason, from disease of the mind." From the time of *M'Naghten* until today some finding of "mental disease or defect" has been a necessary predicate for the insanity defense.

> Second, once such a "disease" is shown, the inquiry focuses on what the defendant was able to "know." That is, the interest of the law under this test is in the ability of the defendant to "know" certain things. It is for this reason that the inquiry is sometimes referred to as a "cognitive" formula.

> Third, the *M'Naghten* test focuses on two things the defendant must be able to "know" in order to be guilty of a crime. One is "the nature and quality of the act" that was committed. The other is that the act "was wrong." In both instances the question is whether the defendant was "capable" of knowing these things, that is, whether the mental illness had deprived the defendant of the capacity to know what "normal" people are able to know about their behavior. The idea, in sum, is that people who are unable to know the nature of their conduct or who are unable to know that their conduct is wrong are not proper subjects for criminal punishment. In common sense terms, such people should not be regarded as morally responsible for their behavior.

[g] Most commentary on the M'Naghten case proceeds on the assumption that he was mentally ill and that his crime was related to his delusions. However, one author has presented strong evidence in support of the proposition that M'Naghten was not delusional and that his attempt to assassinate the Tory Prime Minister was "a purposeful act of political criminality." Richard Moran, *Knowing Right From Wrong* (1981).

[h] She had been the target of assassination attempts three times in the preceding two years, and one of her attackers had also won an insanity acquittal.

3. The Meaning of "Know" and "Wrong." The *M'Naghten* formula quickly became the accepted approach to the insanity defense in England and in the United States. Indeed, it prevails in England to this day, and has inspired at least a part of the test for the insanity defense in virtually all American jurisdictions ever since its announcement in 1843. Its use over the years, however, has revealed a central ambiguity that became important in the trial of John Hinckley. The concern is with the breadth of the *M'Naghten* test, and specifically with the meaning that should be assigned to the words "know" and "wrong."

(i) **"Know."** Consider first the word "know." The question is whether this word is to be given purely cognitive meaning or whether it is to be given a more "affective" meaning (as mental health professionals would describe it). "Know" in the purely cognitive sense asks whether the defendant is able to perceive correctly certain objective features of behavior. "Know" in the latter "affective" sense asks whether the defendant is able fully to "appreciate" the significance of cognitive observations, that is, whether the defendant is able to relate what is "known" to the situation at hand and to govern conduct accordingly.

To illustrate the difference, Daniel M'Naghten probably knew the nature and wrongfulness of his conduct in a purely cognitive sense. He "knew" that he was firing a gun at another person (he did not believe that the victim was a cow, for example) and he probably "knew," at some level of awareness, that shooting other people was against the law and that he would be arrested and prosecuted for such behavior. But, if "know" is given an "affective" content, one would also ask whether M'Naghten was able to "internalize" his cognitive "knowledge" and was able to govern his behavior accordingly. From this "affective" perspective, M'Naghten might not have fully "appreciated" the significance of his conduct at the time he acted because of his overwhelming feeling that he had to put an end to the persecution he was suffering at Tory hands. If this feature of M'Naghten's illness is taken into account, it could be said that what he "knew" in a purely cognitive sense was actually irrelevant to him, psychologically speaking, at the time he acted.

Obviously, this second meaning of "know" is subtle, indeterminate, and hard to measure. It is more generous to defendants in the sense that it opens more avenues for testimony about the effect of mental illness on the controls that the defendant is capable of exercising over conduct. By contrast, the purely "cognitive" inquiry is very strict. Very few defendants who are able to walk around and take care of themselves misperceive the physical features of the world or fail to realize that their conduct will be viewed as wrong by accepted social standards.

(ii) **"Wrong."** A second ambiguity in the *M'Naghten* formula concerns the meaning of the word "wrong." The term could be defined in a narrow sense to mean "crime." Under this restrictive approach, the question would be whether the defendant knew or was able to know that certain behavior was a crime. It would not matter, for example, if a defendant deludedly thought that divine forces commanded that the victim be shot, so long as it was known that it was against the law to shoot the victim. M'Naghten's delusion probably would not have mattered under the definition of "wrong" as "crime" because it did not affect his capacity to know that his act was wrong. Even if his delusions had been true (that is, even if the Tories had been persecuting him), his act would still have been a crime. Fear of persecution is not a legal justification for murder. In short, M'Naghten probably knew enough about his conduct to be able to know that it was a crime.

However, the term "wrong" can also be given a broader meaning. It could be defined to take into account the defendant's own idiosyncratic beliefs about the desirability of certain behavior. In M'Naghten's case, for example, it could be argued that his moral vision had been distorted by his mental illness. He thought he was doing the "right" thing because, in his deluded state, he thought the Prime Minister was the evil leader of a Tory conspiracy to persecute him. From this perspective, it could be said that M'Naghten did not understand that his conduct was "wrong."

Note finally that it is possible to combine the broad concept of "affective" knowledge with this broad, individualized concept of "wrong." If this is done, the *M'Naghten* test has been extended well beyond general awareness of the physical character of one's conduct and its legal significance. Such an approach also takes into account distortions of insight or judgment that dilute or attenuate the person's understanding of the nature and full significance of her or his actions. Those who support this broadened version of the test argue that such an approach is necessary in order to take into account the morally relevant features of serious mental illness. As one commentator has put it, the defense of insanity is appropriate when the defendant:

> is so detached from the external world that he views the significance of his conduct solely, or primarily, through the prism of his own distorted intrapsychic processes, and [when] there is a corresponding loss of ability to recognize and identify with the interests of others in a way that would be expected to illuminate the conduct's wrongfulness and thus operate to deter it.[i]

Consider also the following comments from Gregory Zilboorg, Misconceptions of Legal Insanity, 9 Am.J.Orthopsychiat. 540, 552–553 (1939):*

[i] Richard Bonnie, Morality, Equality and Expertise: Renegotiating the Relationship Between Psychiatry and the Criminal Law, 12 Bull.Amer.Acad. of Psychiat. and Law 5 (1984).

* Reprinted with permission from the American Journal of Orthopsychiatry, copyright 1939 by the American Orthopsychiatry Association, Inc.

The law automatically assumes that a child committing a felony does not know the nature and quality of the act and does not know that it is wrong. Yet a child of moderate brightness will say that he hit his sister on the head, that she bled and then she fell; he will even admit that she died or that he killed her and perhaps will say that he was wrong to kill his sister. The criminal code does not accept this knowledge as valid; without knowing it, the law itself recognizes here a fundamental medico-psychological distinction between the purely verbal knowledge which characterizes the child and the other type of knowledge which characterizes the adult. The fundamental difference between verbal or purely intellectual knowledge and the mysterious other kind of knowledge is familiar to every clinical psychiatrist; it is the difference between knowledge divorced from affect and knowledge so fused with affect that it becomes a human reality. . . .

Therefore "defect of reason" which the law stresses may not ... lie within the field of reason at all, but within the field of emotional appreciation. This emotional appreciation is a very complex phenomenon. It is based on a series of intricate psychological mechanisms. . . . [Without it,] the impulse breaks through and fear of the law and sense of wrong is paled, devoid of its affective component; it becomes a verbal, coldly intellectual, formal, childish, infantile psychological presentation.

4. Other Early Formulations. Nineteenth century authorities offered two alternatives to *M'Naghten*. One is the so-called "irresistible impulse" test, which has had a considerable impact on the formulation of the insanity defense. The other is usually called the "product" test, which has not been widely adopted but which was, for a time, the rule in the District of Columbia.

(i) The "Irresistible Impulse" Test. Although the notion of "irresistible impulse" was much discussed after *M'Naghten*,[j] it is not altogether clear whether the early proponents viewed "irresistible impulse" as an elaboration of *M'Naghten* or as an independent ground of defense. Some state courts employed the concept simply to acknowledge that an "insane impulse" could be so strong as to "dethrone reason" and thereby deprive the offender of the capacity to know that what she or he was doing was wrong.[k] In this sense, therefore, the doctrine still required

---

[j] See generally Sheldon Glueck, Mental Disorder and the Criminal Law (1925); John Barker Waite, Irresistible Impulse and Criminal Liability, 23 Mich.L.Rev. 443 (1925).

[k] See, e.g., Commonwealth v. Rogers, 48 Mass. (7 Metc.) 500, 41 Am.Dec. 458 (1844).

For a review of the early decisions, see Jerome Hall, Psychiatry and Criminal Responsibility, 65 Yale L.J. 761 (1956); Edwin Keedy, Irresistible Impulse as a Defense in the Criminal Law, 100 U.Pa.L.Rev. 956 (1952).

that the *M'Naghten* questions be asked and provided no defense unless the defendant was insane under the *M'Naghten* standard.

However, the phrase "irresistible impulse" ultimately came to denote an independent defense, a defense that might exonerate even if the defendant were sane under *M'Naghten*. Sir James Stephen, a prominent English judge and legal historian, became a leading proponent of an independent "irresistible impulse" defense. In 1883 he stated:

> If it is not, it ought to be the law of England that no act is a crime if the person who does it is at the time ... prevented either by defective mental power or by any disease affecting his mind from controlling his own conduct, unless the absence of the power of control has been produced by his own default.[1]

The first unequivocal American endorsement of such a formulation is found in Parsons v. State, 81 Ala. 577, 596, 2 So. 854, 866 (1887):

> [D]id he know right from wrong, as applied to the particular act in question? ... If he did have such knowledge, he may nevertheless not be legally responsible if the following conditions occur: (i) if by reason of the duress of such mental disease, he had so far lost the *power to choose* between the right and wrong, and to avoid doing the act in question, as that his free agency was at the time destroyed; (ii) and if, at the same time, the alleged crime was so connected with such mental disease, in the relation of cause and effect, as to have been the product of it *solely*.

Although several other courts endorsed this view during the next decade, most rejected it. The attitude of the courts that rejected it was explained by a Canadian judge in 1908:

> The law says to men who say they are afflicted with irresistible impulses: "If you cannot resist an impulse in any other way, we will hang a rope in front of your eyes, and perhaps that will help." No man has a right under our law to come before a jury and say to them, "I did commit that act, but I did it under an uncontrollable impulse," leave it at that and then say, "now acquit me."[m]

Many others have echoed these sentiments. Additionally, they have argued that a defense stated in these terms is impractical because mental health professionals are not able to determine whether a crime was committed because the defendant *did not* exercise self-control or because the defendant *could not* have done so.

In any event, the central focus of the "irresistible impulse" idea is on the ability of the defendant to exercise self-control. The inquiry, which has come to be known as a "volitional" or "control" test, is

---

[1] 2 James F. Stephen, A History of the Criminal Law of England 168 (1883).

[m] King v. Creighton, 14 Can.Cr.Cases 349, 350 (1908).

whether, as a result of mental disease or defect, the defendant had lost the capacity to control behavior, that is, whether the defendant could have chosen not to commit the crime.

The common-sense theory underlying this idea is not difficult to understand. It rests on the notion, referred to above, that the conviction of crime expresses a moral judgment about the defendant's behavior. Moral judgments about people, the argument goes, are premised on the concept of free will. In general, behavior is the product of choice, and people who make bad choices are subject to moral condemnation. In cases where mental disease or defect robs people of the capacity to choose not to engage in criminal behavior, the argument concludes, it is inappropriate to condemn them morally and therefore inappropriate to convict them of a crime.

The difference between *M'Naghten* and "irresistible impulse" as a criterion for stating the content of the insanity defense, then, concerns the questions that should be asked about the defendant's psychological functioning at the time of the offense. Both inquiries are based on a determination that the defendant suffers from incapacitating mental disease. The difference between them turns on the effect of the disease on the defendant's behavior:

> *M'Naghten* asks whether mental illness has eroded the defendant's capacity to understand the nature of behavior and its moral context. It is premised on the theory that people who can understand the nature and moral significance of their behavior will be in a position to make proper choices about what to do and what not to do. When people are "normal" in the sense that they can understand these things, they can properly be punished by the criminal law if they choose to commit a crime.

> By contrast, the "irresistible impulse" test asks whether mental illness has compromised the defendant's capacity to control behavior. When people are "normal" in the sense that they have the capacity to exercise behavioral controls, they can properly be punished by the criminal law if they fail to do so.

(ii) The Product Test. *M'Naghten* was criticized by Isaac Ray[n] and his followers because it failed to take into account the more subtle forms of mental illness. The prevailing judicial ideas about idiocy and lunacy were derived, Ray argued, from "those wretched inmates of the madhouses whom chains and stripes, cold and filth, had reduced to the stupidity of the idiot or exasperated to the fury of a demon." The law failed to recognize "those nice shades of the disease" that can influence behavior and that ought to be recognized as a defense to crime. Accordingly, Ray argued, the insanity defense should be broadened and should

---

[n] Isaac Ray, A Treatise on the Medical Jurisprudence of Insanity (1838).

turn on whether "mental unsoundness ... embraced the act within the sphere of its influence."

The New Hampshire Supreme Court accepted Ray's view. In State v. Pike, 49 N.H. 399 (1870), the court severely criticized the *M'Naghten* rules. The next year, in State v. Jones, 50 N.H. 369 (1871), the court stated its own rule, which has come to be known as the "product" test:

> No man shall be held accountable, criminally, for an act which was the offspring and product of mental disease. Of the soundness of this proposition there can be no doubt.... No argument is needed to show that to hold that a man may be punished for what is the offspring of disease would be to hold that he may be punished for disease. Any rule which makes that possible cannot be law.

Although the New Hampshire formulation was applauded by many medical and legal commentators during the early part of the 20th century, it failed to win support in the courts. It has been adopted in no other state, although, as developed more fully below, it was used in the District of Columbia for 18 years.

Note that both of the previously discussed insanity tests ask a version of the "product" question. Both *M'Naghten* and "irresistible impulse" require that the particular characteristics on which they focus must be a "product" of the defendant's mental disease—that is, the disease must have caused the defendant to have been unable to know right from wrong or to have been unable to control behavior. The difference is that the "product" test asks a more direct question, namely whether the defendant's conduct itself was the "product" of mental illness. In a sense, *M'Naghten* and "irresistible impulse" suggest that particular symptoms caused by disease should control the inquiry that the law should make. The "product" formula asks only whether the crime was caused by the defendant's mental illness.

Adoption of the "product" test by the New Hampshire Supreme Court was based on the court's assumption that serious forms of mental illness are analogous to physical diseases. To punish a person with pneumonia for coughing or to punish an epileptic for a seizure would be unthinkable. So too, the court reasoned, it is morally inappropriate to punish a person for behavior that is caused in the same sense by a mental disease.

It is difficult to quarrel with the moral supposition underlying the court's reasoning. The "product" test has not been widely used, however, for a number of reasons. Criticism of the test has focused in part on the court's empirical premise—that is, on the idea that mental disease "causes" behavior in the same sense that epilepsy "causes" seizures. It is now generally recognized that behavior controls are variably affected by different forms of mental illness in different individuals. It is not true to say that a mentally ill person has as little control over conduct "symptomatic" of the "disease" as an epileptic has over whether to have a seizure. The law is thus not relieved from the difficult task of drawing a moral line between behavior so closely related to mental illness as to have been "produced" by that illness and behavior over which the person still retained sufficient control as to be legally responsible. The "product" test does not, in other words, make the job of the law any less difficult.

In fact, it makes the job more difficult. Once it is established in a criminal trial that the defendant suffered from a mental disease, it is difficult for the jury to conclude that the disease was unrelated to the defendant's behavior. Thus, in an important sense, the most significant issue in a trial under the New Hampshire formulation is whether the defendant suffers from a mental illness. Those who reject the "product" test believe that there are some people who suffer from mental illness who nonetheless should be judged morally responsible for their behavior. It is the challenge in formulating an insanity defense, they argue, to describe such people and to exclude them from the defense. This the "product" test does not do.

5. The Model Penal Code. The formative era of the modern insanity defense was completed by the end of the 19th century. Notwithstanding a persistent barrage of unfavorable commentary by forensic psychiatrists and academic lawyers, the law remained essentially unchanged for the first half of the 20th century. The *M'Naghten* test still constituted the exclusive version of the insanity defense in about two-thirds of the states. One state, New Hampshire, followed the "product" test. And the remaining states supplemented *M'Naghten* with the additional "control" inquiry supplied by the "irresistible impulse" formula.

Prior to the *Hinckley* case, the most important development in the history of the insanity defense in this century was the drafting of the Model Penal Code. The Model Penal Code, as its name implies, was a statute designed to be used as a model for legislation around the country. It was written by the American Law Institute, an influential organization composed of lawyers, judges, and academics supported by private funding. The Model Code was begun in 1952 and completed in 1962.

The Model Penal Code has had an enormous impact on the development of American criminal law in many areas, and its insanity test was especially influential. By 1980, the Model Code insanity defense had been adopted—by legislation or by judicial ruling—in more than half the states. Moreover, Congress had never addressed the proper content of the insanity defense. In the absence of legislative action, the Model Code formulation had been adopted by all of the federal courts of appeal.

Section 4.01(1) of the Model Code states the insanity defense as follows:

> A person is not responsible for criminal conduct if at the time of such conduct as a result of mental disease or defect he

lacks substantial capacity either to appreciate the criminality
[wrongfulness] of his conduct or to conform his conduct to the
requirements of law.

The Model Code continues the tradition of earlier insanity tests by
requiring that the defendant suffer from a "mental disease or defect." It
then asks questions about how that mental disease affected the defendant at the time of the offense. Three points should be noted about these
questions:

First, the Model Code is an amalgam of *M'Naghten* and "irresistible impulse." It contains a "cognitive" inquiry, which asks
about the defendant's capacity "to appreciate the criminality
[wrongfulness] of his conduct."[o] It also contains a "volitional" or
"control" inquiry, which asks about the defendant's capacity "to
conform his conduct to the requirements of law." Because these
questions are separated by an "or," the defendant has a defense if
either of these criteria are satisfied.

Second, the Model Code asks whether the defendant lacked
"substantial" capacity to appreciate wrongfulness or exercise control. *M'Naghten* had asked whether the defendant was *completely*
incapable of knowing right from wrong and the traditional "irresistible impulse" test had asked whether the defendant was *completely*
incapable of exercising control. The word "substantial" was included
in the Model Penal Code to acknowledge that there is no bright line
between the sane and the insane. In the words of Professor Herbert
Wechsler, who inspired the Model Code language, "what clinical
experience revealed was closer to a graded scale with marks along
the way."[p] Accordingly, he continued, "it was thought that the

[o] Notice that this part of the Model Penal
Code test asks only one of the M'Naghten
questions. Section 4.01(1) of the Model Penal Code omits reference to the capacity of
the defendant to "know the nature and
quality of the act" that he or she was
committing. There are two reasons for this
omission.

The first is that the significance of a
person's mistake regarding the nature of
conduct lies ultimately in the fact that it
prevents her or him from knowing that it is
wrong. One cannot know that behavior is
wrong if one is incapable of knowing the
nature of the behavior itself. Thus, this part
of the M'Naghten test can be regarded as
superfluous, and was so regarded by the
drafters of the Model Penal Code.

Second, this aspect of the M'Naghten formula is directed primarily to the capacity of
the defendant to form the "intent" required for conviction of a criminal offense.
Most crimes, certainly all serious crimes,

require for conviction that the defendant
"know" certain legally relevant circumstances relating to her or his conduct, that
the defendant intend to perform certain
actions, or that the defendant intend to
accomplish certain results. The highest cat-
egory of murder in a given jurisdiction, for
example, is likely to require that the defendant "intend to kill another person." Another provision of the Model Penal Code
permits evidence of mental illness to be
admitted whenever it is relevant to the
existence or nonexistence of a state of mind
of this sort. Thus, evidence that, because of
mental illness, the defendant was unable to
"know the nature and quality of the act"
will be admitted anyway, making the separate asking of this question as part of the
insanity test redundant.

[p] Herbert Wechsler, Codification of the
Criminal Law in the United States: The
Model Penal Code, 68 Colum.L.Rev. 1425,
1443 (1968).

criterion should ask if there was, as a result of disease or defect, a deprivation of 'substantial capacity' to know or to control, meaning thereby the reduction of capacity to the vagrant and trivial dimensions characteristic of the most severe afflictions of the mind."

Third, the Model Code uses the term "appreciate" instead of "know" in the *M'Naghten* part of its formula. This reintroduces the debate under *M'Naghten* about whether the Model Code means to adopt a purely "cognitive" inquiry or whether it means to ask "affective" questions instead. As will be seen, this aspect of the Model Code formulation became particularly important in the trial of John Hinckley.

6. The Insanity Defense in the District of Columbia. John Hinckley was tried in a federal court in the District of Columbia. Two aspects of the insanity defense applicable in the District at that time should be noted.

(i) The Insanity Test. Until 1954, the District of Columbia followed *M'Naghten* supplemented by "irresistible impulse." Then, in a famous decision, Durham v. United States, 214 F.2d 862 (D.C.Cir.1954), the "product" test was adopted for the District. This test was used until 1972, when in United States v. Brawner, 471 F.2d 969 (D.C.Cir.1972), the court abandoned the "product" test in favor of the Model Penal Code insanity formula. Thus, the insanity defense applicable to the *Hinckley* case followed the language suggested in the Model Penal Code.

(ii) The Concept of "Mental Disease." Recall that all formulations of the insanity defense require as a threshold condition that the defendant be suffering from a "mental disease or defect." There has been over the years considerable debate about what kinds of mental conditions should qualify as a "mental disease or defect" for this purpose. Some have contended[q] that the concept should be limited to the kinds of gross disturbance of mental functioning commonly referred to as psychoses.[r] Others have taken the position that the requirement of a "mental disease or defect" should not operate as an independent limita-

[q] See, e.g., Royal Commission on Capital Punishment, Report 73 (1953); Joseph Livermore and Paul Meehl, the Virtues of M'Naghten, 51 Minn.L.Rev. 789, 831–32 (1967).

[r] According to the glossary of the fourth edition of the Diagnostic and Statistical Manual of the American Psychiatric Association (DSM–IV) the meaning of the term "psychotic" varies somewhat in relation to particular disorders. However, the "narrowest definition" is restricted to delusions or prominent hallucinations in the absence of insight into their pathological nature. Conceptually, the term refers to a "gross impairment in reality testing":

When there is gross impairment in reality testing, the individual incorrectly evaluates the accuracy of his or her perceptions and thoughts and makes incorrect inferences about external reality, even in the face of contrary evidence. The term psychotic does not apply to minor distortions of reality that involve matters of relative judgment. For example, a depressed person who underestimated his achievements would not be described as a psychotic, whereas one who believed he had caused a natural catastrophe would be so described.

tion on the availability of the insanity defense.[s] Most views, however, fall somewhere in between these two extremes.

The approach to this question in the District of Columbia was first stated in McDonald v. United States, 312 F.2d 847, 851 (D.C.Cir.1962), where the court took an intermediate position, defining mental disease as "any abnormal condition of the mind which substantially affects mental or emotional processes and substantially impairs behavior controls." The court reaffirmed this definition when it endorsed the Model Code approach in United States v. Brawner, 471 F.2d 969 (D.C.Cir. 1972).[t] It was this definition, therefore, that was applicable when John Hinckley was tried.

7.   The *Hinckley* Case. Signs of dissatisfaction with the prevailing approach to the insanity defense began to emerge in the late 1970's. One major factor was public concern about premature release of dangerous defendants who had been acquitted by reason of insanity. During this period, several states narrowed the insanity criteria. One state, Montana, abolished a separate insanity defense altogether (in 1979). The simmering debate about the insanity defense took on national proportions in reaction to the *Hinckley* trial. The dimensions of this debate will be summarized after consideration of the *Hinckley* case itself.

---

[s] See, e.g., Judge Bazelon's position, which was not adopted by the court, in United States v. Brawner, 471 F.2d 969, 1010–39 (D.C.Cir.1972).

[t] It is generally recognized that the Durham experiment in the District of Columbia failed in large measure because of the elasticity of the concept of mental disease. In this respect, the "product" test employed in the District under Durham had little in common with the "product" test envisioned by Isaac Ray and the New Hampshire Supreme Court a century earlier. When originally articulated, the "product" test was clearly tied to the "disease" model of mental illness described above. The New Hampshire court assumed that the concept of "mental disease" would keep the boundaries of the defense confined to the same class of severely disturbed persons contemplated by courts using the M'Naghten and "irresistible impulse" tests. The court was aiming not to broaden the class of persons entitled to raise the defense, but rather to broaden the dimensions of the inquiry so as to take into account the full clinical picture in cases of major mental illness.

By contrast, when the Durham decision was announced in 1954, the "disease" model of mental illness no longer represented the prevailing clinical perspective. Instead, concepts of mental abnormality were heavily influenced by the "dimensional" and "psychological explanation" perspectives discussed above. As applied in the District of Columbia, the "product" test opened the door to claims of insanity for any defendant who could be characterized as having a "mental disorder" under the elastic definitions of that concept used by the mental health disciplines. For this reason, the litigation of insanity defenses in the District of Columbia often turned on arguments about what constituted a mental disorder. Moreover, because the insanity test asked only whether the defendant's conduct was a "product" of the mental disorder, the expert testimony was often characterized by unstructured clinical speculation about the "causes" of the defendant's behavior.

*

PART II

The *Hinckley* Trial

UNITED STATES v. JOHN W. HINCKLEY, JR.

United States District Court for the District of Columbia, 1982.
Criminal Case no. 81–306.

1. Introduction. As noted above, the transcript of the *Hinckley* trial consumes 7,342 pages. The defense introduced testimony by four experts who evaluated Hinckley after the shooting and also called Hinckley's mother, father, other members of the family, and a psychiatrist who had been treating Hinckley prior to the shooting. The prosecution called a number of lay witnesses, who described Hinckley's behavior during the days immediately before and after the offense, and two psychiatrists who evaluated him afterwards.

Materials drawn from the transcript of the *Hinckley* trial appear in the following pages. These materials have been presented in three parts: first, narrative summaries of, and excerpts from, the expert testimony; second, excerpts from the closing arguments of the prosecution and defense; and third, relevant portions of the instructions delivered to the jury by the presiding judge, Barrington T. Parker.

2. The Expert Testimony. The experts who evaluated John Hinckley and testified at his trial had conflicting opinions concerning the nature and severity of his mental disorder, and drew significantly divergent inferences concerning his mental condition at the time of the offense. However, these disagreements should not obscure important areas of agreement about Hinckley's condition and about many clinically significant symptoms.

The following summary of the testimony describes these areas of agreement and highlights the areas of dispute as they relate to the ongoing controversy about the scope of the insanity defense. It must be emphasized, however, that this summary does not cover all relevant issues, nor does it reflect the relative strengths and weaknesses of the opposing positions. Only a narrative of much greater length could do so.

The testimony is presented in four sections: first, a summary of the undisputed data—both observed and self-reported—concerning Hinckley's behavior from the fall of 1973, when he enrolled in college, to March, 1981, when he attempted to kill the President; second, a summary of the testimony relating to the nature and severity of Hinckley's mental disorder, together with excerpts[a] concerning two significant areas of clinical disagreement; third, portions of the expert testimony concerning Hinckley's capacity to appreciate the wrongfulness of his conduct; and fourth, portions of the expert testimony concerning his capacity to conform his conduct to the requirements of the law.

(i) **Hinckley's Behavior.** To a large extent, the expert opinions were based on the same sources of data—interviews with Hinckley, who was both able and willing to describe his feelings and motivations in considerable detail; interviews with his parents, siblings and others who observed him; and numerous poems, stories, and letters which Hinckley wrote, and books and movies which he had read or seen, during the critical period preceding the offense. The prosecution and defense experts differed in the extent of their reliance on these various sources. For example, the defense relied heavily on Hinckley's own accounts and on his writings, while the prosecution experts saw evidence of manipulation in Hinckley's own descriptions, tended to discount the clinical significance of his writings, and relied more heavily on the physical evidence relating to the shootings. By and large, however, the experts based their opinions on the same reconstruction of Hinckley's behavior from the time he enrolled in college through the period preceding the effort to kill the President.

Hinckley began to exhibit a tendency toward social withdrawal during adolescence. He did not date and had difficulty establishing peer relationships. After enrolling at Texas Tech, in Lubbock, in the fall of 1973, he reportedly spent much of his time for the next two years reading, watching television, listening to music, and playing the guitar. He apparently established no meaningful personal relationships outside of his family. In the spring of 1976, he dropped out of school and went to Hollywood, where he spent six months in futile pursuit of a career as a songwriter.

While in Hollywood, he became intensely interested in the movie "Taxi Driver," which he saw about 15 times. In this movie, Robert DeNiro portrayed the central character, Travis Bickle, an alienated, violent taxi driver who became interested in a woman (Betsy) who worked for a presidential candidate. When he was unsuccessful in his efforts to establish a relationship with her, Bickle decided to assassinate the presidential candidate. After being thwarted in this effort, he turned his attention toward "rescuing" Iris, a young prostitute played by Jodie Foster. Eventually Bickle was perceived as a hero for rescuing Iris after a fatal shootout with her pimp.

---

[a] All excerpts have been organized topically rather than chronologically. Accordingly they do not appear in the order in which the testimony was presented. The testimony has also been edited for obvious errors in transcription or punctuation. In some instances, paragraphs have been combined or separated to improve the clarity of the materials. Lengthy deletions are indicated by ellipses or by the substitution of bracketed language. In making these editorial improvements, every effort has been made to preserve the speaker's intended meaning.

According to Dr. William Carpenter, Jr., one of the defense experts, Hinckley "identified" with Travis Bickle and "picked up in largely automatic ways many [of his] attributes." Dr. Carpenter found many similarities—for example, Hinckley began wearing an army fatigue jacket and keeping a diary, and became fascinated with guns. In Carpenter's opinion, this process, which was mainly an unconscious one, occurred because Hinckley's emotional isolation and poorly developed sense of identity made him especially "vulnerable" and "open to influences" at this time. The prosecution experts agreed that Hinckley imitated Travis Bickle in some respects, but resisted the conclusion that he lost his own identity and absorbed Bickle's.

According to Dr. Carpenter, Hinckley also developed an "enormous interest" in Jodie Foster which ultimately became an obsession. Of more immediate importance in 1976 was Betsy, the object of Bickle's frustrated attention. Hinckley fabricated a girlfriend named Lynn, modeled after Betsy, whom he described in his letters to his parents. He did this in order to show his parents that he was maturing and to persuade them to continue to support his futile effort to launch a career as a songwriter. Eventually, he reported that he and Lynn had a falling-out, admitted that his career was stillborn, and returned to the family home in Evergreen, Colorado, in the fall of 1976.

After living alone in an apartment and working as a busboy during the winter, Hinckley made another unsuccessful trip to Hollywood in the spring of 1977. He then reenrolled at Texas Tech, and remained in Lubbock until the winter of 1979–80. During this period, Hinckley apparently attended class only sporadically and spent much of his time alone. This was a period of intensifying conflict with his parents over his poor school performance and his failure to establish acceptable occupational goals. According to the defense experts, he became severely depressed during this period, feeling "aimless" and "that there was no purpose to his life." His letters to his parents include renewed references to "Lynn," who supposedly visited him in Lubbock and supported his desire for an artistic career. In August, 1979, he purchased his first gun and began target-shooting.

Hinckley spent Christmas of 1979 alone in Lubbock because, according to Dr. Carpenter, "he didn't feel he could go home and face up to the effort of trying to relate to members of his family." A self-taken photograph during early 1980 shows Hinckley, considerably overweight, holding a gun to his temple. Although Hinckley said that the gun was not loaded at the time of this photograph, he did report to Dr. Carpenter that he had played "Russian Roulette" on at least two occasions in November and December.

In early 1980, Hinckley returned to Evergreen for medical examinations arranged by his parents in response to his complaints of sleeplessness, headaches, and physical weakness. The physicians found no physical explanation for his ailments and concluded that they were probably symptomatic expressions of anxiety or stress. His parents became increasingly frustrated with their son's aimlessness and failure to pursue "reasonable goals" and arranged for him to see a psychologist employed by his father's firm in August, 1980. The upshot of this family visit was that Hinckley declared a new goal of pursuing a writing career, and requested that his parents subsidize his enrollment in a writing course being offered at Yale. In a written agreement executed on September 16, 1980, he promised, in exchange for $3,600, to work productively at Yale and, in the event that his new career did not work out, to re-enroll at Texas Tech in the fall.

Hinckley left the next day for New Haven. However, he apparently had no intention of taking a writing course. Instead, his purpose was to establish contact with Jodie Foster, who had recently begun her first year of undergraduate study at Yale. He left letters and poems in her mailbox and had two awkward telephone conversations with her which he recorded.

Disappointed in his efforts to establish a relationship with Jodie Foster, Hinckley left New Haven, and after a stop in Denver, flew to Lubbock, where he purchased two .22 handguns, giving him a total of three handguns and two rifles. He then decided to stalk President Carter. Hinckley traveled to Washington, D.C., Columbus, Ohio, and Dayton, Ohio, over a three-day period. On October 2, he actually went where Carter was making a campaign appearance, although he left his weapons in his hotel room. According to Dr. Carpenter, Hinckley "felt he was just unable to get himself into a frame of mind where he could actually carry out the act [of assassination] at that time."

Hinckley then returned to New Haven, leaving more notes for Jodie Foster, and flew to Lincoln, Nebraska on October 6. The purpose of this trip, according to Dr. Carpenter was to establish contact with "one of the leading ideologicians" of the American Nazi Party. No such meeting occurred and Hinckley traveled the next day to Nashville, where President Carter was making a campaign stop. When Hinckley went to the airport on October 9, the security staff confiscated the handguns and handcuffs detected in his suitcase and arrested him. He paid a fine and did not try to reclaim the guns. After a two-day stop in New Haven, Hinckley traveled to Dallas, where he visited his sister and purchased two more .22 handguns, returned to New Haven, and then went to Washington, apparently in continued pursuit of Carter.

Hinckley was by now running out of money and flew to his parents' home in Evergreen on October 20. His parents expressed disappointment in his failure to carry out his promises and became increasingly concerned about his mental health. While at home, Hinckley apparently took an overdose of valium or antidepressant medication, or at least led his parents to think he had done so, whereupon they arranged an appointment with a local psychiatrist, Dr. John Hopper.

During the next four months, Hinckley met with Dr. Hopper periodically. It appears from Dr. Hopper's testimony, as well as from Hinckley's statements to the experts who later examined him, that he was very guarded in his sessions with Dr. Hopper. He did not mention his guns, his stalking, his assassination plans, or his fascination with *Taxi Driver*. His only mention of Jodie Foster was apparently in an autobiographical sketch he had prepared at Dr. Hopper's request, in which he stated that all he cared about were a writing career and Jodie Foster. Eventually, Dr. Hopper, Hinckley, and his parents agreed that Hinckley should get a job by the end of February, as the first step in a plan to achieve financial and emotional independence from his parents.

During the course of his treatment, Hinckley continued to crisscross the country. On November 30, he went to Washington, D.C., where President-elect Reagan was staying. When he learned about the death of rock singer John Lennon, he was, according to Dr. Carpenter, "stunned," and he went to New York to join others who were mourning Lennon's death. After a brief trip to New Haven on December 15, where he left more poems and notes for Jodie Foster, he returned to Colorado for the Christmas holidays. In a tape-recorded monologue, which he apparently made while intoxicated on New Year's eve, he expressed fears that he was on the road to "insanity," and described his frustrated longing for Jodie Foster. At one point he said it would be "suicide city" if he failed to win her affection and, at another, he said "I don't really want to hurt her."

Between February 9 and February 19, Hinckley traveled back and forth between New Haven, Washington, and New York. While in New York, he went to "the Dakota," the apartment building in front of which Lennon had been shot. Hinckley told various experts that he had contemplated killing himself in the same spot where Lennon had been killed but was unable to pull out the weapon and shoot himself. Although the prosecution and defense experts disagreed on the content and intensity of Hinckley's ruminations during this period, they did agree that he was at least preoccupied with Jodie Foster and with assassination—preoccupations reflected in his reading of books on assassinations, in the poems he was writing, and in the notes he was sending to Jodie Foster.

Hinckley returned to Evergreen on February 19. His parents were out of town. He had his last appointment with Dr. Hopper on February 27. Having failed to get a job by the end of February, as he had promised, he wanted to avoid a confrontation with his parents, so he left on March 1, before they returned. He then went to New York and New Haven, leaving Jodie Foster several love notes, one of which stated:

"Jodie, after tonight John Lennon and I will have a lot in common. It's all for you."

On March 5, having run out of money, he called his parents and pleaded with them to permit him to come home. His father paid for his trip home, but when he arrived at the airport on March 7, his father said that, in keeping with their agreement, he would not permit his son to come home. Instead, Hinckley's father gave him money and suggested that he stay at the YMCA. Between March 7 and March 25, Hinckley stayed at two motels in the Denver vicinity, spending most of his time alone watching television and reading. Unbeknownst to his father, he visited his mother at the family home and picked up some of his belongings there. To raise money, he sold several of his guns and other possessions.

Hinckley then decided to go to Hollywood for one last effort to sell his songs. He had told his mother about his plan, and she agreed to drive him to the airport. According to both Hinckley and his mother, the drive was made in virtual silence and with a shared sense that his relationship with his parents was being terminated. After one day in Hollywood, Hinckley boarded a bus to Washington, where he arrived on March 29 and checked into the Park Central Hotel. The next day he wrote a letter to Jodie Foster describing his assassination plan, went to the Hilton, and attempted to kill President Reagan.

(ii) Hinckley's Mental Disorder. All of the experts who evaluated Hinckley agreed that his behavior included symptoms of psychological disturbance. However, the defense and prosecution witnesses drew different inferences concerning the nature and severity of his disorder. The defense experts detected a serious deterioration of his condition, as evidenced by a progressive withdrawal into his "inner world" as his "anchors" to reality slipped away. Although the defense witnesses did not agree on the precise diagnosis, they all testified that Hinckley was psychotic at the time of the offense.

According to Dr. Carpenter, Hinckley met the criteria for schizophrenia under the American Psychiatric Association's Diagnostic and Statistical Manual, Third Edition (DSM–III).[b] In support of the diagnosis, Dr. Carpenter stated that Hinckley exhibited four major symptoms or manifestations of mental illness: "blunted affect," which refers to "an incapacity to have an ordinary emotional arousal that should be associated with events in life"; "autistic retreat from reality" which refers to "the process of pulling into [one's] inner mind and away from outer reality"; depression, including "suicidal features"; and severe impairment of functioning in society, including inability to work or establish social bonds. Dr. Carpenter linked his diagnosis under DSM–III to "a

[b] At the time of Hinckley's trial, DSM–III   DSM–IV.
was in use. It has now been superseded by

more broadly used concept" called "process schizophrenia" which begins "with fairly subtle disorders in social functioning" and "progresses to a more severe . . . psychotic disorder." According to Dr. Thomas Goldman, Hinckley's condition would have been diagnosed as "simple schizophrenia" under the less rigid diagnostic criteria employed by DSM–II. Although Dr. Goldman concluded that Hinckley did not meet the specific criteria for schizophrenia under DSM–III, he said that diagnoses of either "schizotypal personality disorder" or "borderline personality disorder" would be appropriate. He chose the former as his primary diagnosis "to stress the closeness of the clinical picture to forms of schizophrenia" and emphasized, as the "main point," that Hinckley "was in a psychotic state at the time he performed the act."[c]

In contrast, all of the prosecution's experts concluded that Hinckley's condition did *not* meet the criteria for schizophrenia or any other psychotic disorder and that he was *not* psychotic at the time of the offense. Dr. Park Elliott Dietz, presenting the opinions of a four-man team of experts retained by the prosecution, testified that Hinckley met the criteria for "dysthymic disorder" (which he described as "sad mood" disorder), "narcissistic personality disorder" (which he described as "self-centered or self-absorbed personality disorder") and "schizoid personality disorder" (which he said was characterized by lack of friends and emotional coldness or aloofness). He emphasized that these disorders are "considerably less serious" than psychotic disorders and that they are found in a significant percentage of the adult population. He testified, for example, that researchers have estimated that "one out of every 10 to 20 Americans" has dysthymic disorder. The other prosecution expert was Dr. Sally Johnson, the psychiatrist who had conducted the court-ordered evaluation at the Federal Correctional Institute in Butner, N.C., where Hinckley had been hospitalized after his arrest. Her primary diagnosis was "narcissistic personality disorder."

On cross-examination of the defense experts, the government attempted to undermine the diagnosis of psychosis by calling attention to the various ways in which Hinckley was functioning within normal limits and was in touch with social reality—e.g., in his schoolwork when he was enrolled at Texas Tech, in his cross-country travels, and in his dealings with others, including his conversations with Jodie Foster and her roommates.

[c] A third defense psychiatrist, Dr. David Bear, also diagnosed "schizotypal personality disorder" which he described as the DSM–III label for "the man with schizophrenia who [has] all the negative symptoms but [not] the florid positive symptoms." Dr. Ernst Prelinger, a clinical psychologist testified, primarily on the basis of Hinckley's performance on a variety of standard psychological tests, that Hinckley met the criteria for both "borderline personality disorder" and "paranoid personality disorder." Each of the defense experts also noted, with varying degrees of emphasis, that Hinckley's depression was severe enough to support a diagnosis of a "major depressive episode" under DSM–III.

In this connection, the government also introduced testimony of witnesses who had seen Hinckley during the period immediately preceding and following the offense. The maid at the motel where Hinckley stayed between March 8 and March 23 testified that she did not notice any unusual behavior, that he never mentioned Jodie Foster, assassination, or guns, and that Hinckley seemed "just a normal all-American-type boy to me." She also testified that while he was always alone when she saw him, he did not stay in his room all day long.[d] The maid who cleaned Hinckley's room at the Park Central Hotel in Washington just before he left for the Hilton said he "looked calm" and that she did not notice anything unusual. The secret service agent who apprehended Hinckley said he appeared "calm and unemotional" and made no statements suggesting that he was out of contact with reality. The FBI agent who spent some four hours with Hinckley after his arrest testified that the defendant was calm and coherent and carried on normal conversation. Dr. William Brownlee, a surgeon who conducted a physical examination of Hinckley the evening of his arrest testified that Hinckley was "a little bit anxious" and "slightly withdrawn, but not depressed at all" and that "he was not out of touch with reality."

The government also sought to establish doubts about the credibility of some of Hinckley's accounts of his motivation and symptoms by pointing out, for example, that Hinckley described some events that never happened, and that he first reported the "Russian roulette" incidents nine months subsequent to the offense, after the government experts' reports had already been filed. In general, the government sought to emphasize Hinckley's manipulativeness, a characteristic which would explain some of the conduct from which the defense experts inferred the existence of psychosis. One such example was the fabrication of "Lynn" as a tool to persuade his parents to send him money.

In contrast, the defense cross-examination of the government's experts was designed to suggest that their diagnostic conclusions had consistently understated the severity of Hinckley's condition. For example, Dr. Dietz had testified that one of the features of narcissistic personality disorder is a "preoccupation with fantasies of unlimited success and fame." The defense sought to shake this characterization by getting Dr. Dietz to agree that such a preoccupation could also amount to a "grandiose delusion" symptomatic of schizophreniA. Similarly, the prosecution experts had regarded Hinckley's admitted loneliness and social isolation as symptomatic of schizoid personality, and the defense got them to agree that this feature is also commonly associated with schizotypal personality disorder and schizophrenia.

[d] The prosecution experts had also interviewed Richard Park, the person who sat next to Hinckley for about half of his cross-country bus ride to Washington. They testi-fied that, according to Park, Hinckley interacted normally and did not seem either depressed or out of touch with reality.

Perhaps the most significant divergence of clinical opinion about Hinckley's mental disorder at the time of the offense pertained to whether or not Hinckley had "delusions" and "ideas of reference," two key symptoms of psychosis. As the following excerpts from the transcript illustrate, these disagreements reflect differences in clinical inference and characterization rather than disputes about the observable data.

Dr. William T. Carpenter, Jr., Defense Witness

Direct Examination by Defense Attorney Vincent Fuller

Q. [Would you describe the basis for your] diagnos[is] of the defendant's mental illness, mental disease?

A. . . . Delusion is a technical term that refers to the development of a false belief, and a false belief that is not shared by others and is not readily shaken by evidence to the contrary. . . . And it is not simply that it is false that makes it a delusion because people have many false beliefs. But it is false, it is not shared by others, and evidence that would show that it is not, in fact, accurate doesn't shake the belief that the person has. So I use the term "delusion" because it will be important to understand that as a technical judgment that I have made that relates to this withdrawal from reality and the development of the relationship, for example, with Jodie Foster, as it developed over time, took on a quality of a delusion and became delusional. So it was not that it was only a fantasy and a fantasy that became an obsession. It was both of those things. But [he] also developed in that context false beliefs that were not shaken by evidence to the contrary and that, in fact, he was basing many actions of his life on. So that I did conclude that he had developed delusions.

There is another technical term that is important in diagnosis and a symptom that can appear in several different diagnostic categories and that term is "ideas of reference." And this is a technical term that means that a person's mental state is such that they will interpret in a highly personal and idiosyncratic way—that is, a personal and unusual way—what may be common-place events. [M]y conclusion that he had the symptom and manifestation of ideas of reference [comes] from many different examples, some as trivial as like walking down a street and a newspaper blowing across his leg and his giving it some unusual significance or importance that had some actual meaning to him, not just to an event. [Another example is the] personalized quality of when President Reagan was smiling and waving in the crowd in the vicinity where he was, the belief that it had a personal connection.

. . .

Q. [C]an you describe as you understand from Mr. Hinckley his activities of the evening of March 29th and early March 30th?

A.   Yes, when he checked into the Park Central Hotel, he of course was fatigued from the many things, including [the bus ride]. He attempted to rest and sleep during that afternoon, was not able to fall asleep and spent the time reading and watching TV. [He] went out for dinner at a nearby fast-food restaurant, came back to the room and watched TV and then fell asleep that night; that would have been Sunday night, the 29th. [He] described it as a restless fitful sleep that night.

[He] woke up the next morning still feeling fatigued. [He] went out again from the hotel to a nearby fast-food place to get breakfast, picked up a newspaper, returned to his room and in the course of reading the newspaper, he came across itineraries, including President Reagan's itinerary for the day. [He] saw that [the President] was going to be at the Hilton, decided to go to the Hilton and attempt to assassinate President Reagan.

He showered, wrote some material, wrote a letter to Jodie Foster, otherwise prepared himself for ... the plan ... to go to the Hilton. He was not sure [what he would do] in part because there had been a number of other times when he had gone to a place to shoot someone and had been unable to do it. He wasn't sure what the outcome of the trip to the Hilton would be, but he did load his gun.

He had a .22 pistol, loaded his gun, left for the Hilton.

At that point in his mind was the possibility that he might be able to see President Reagan, might be able to attempt the assassination, the possibility that he might proceed that day on to New Haven.... He entertained the possibility he might have to stay another night in Washington and then go to New Haven, so in the course of going to the Hilton, there are still these several possibilities, which includes the possibility of making an assassination attempt.

MR. FULLER: Your Honor, I hand the witness what has been marked Exhibit N–15....

Can you identify that document, Doctor?

A.   Yes. The document, N–15, is a letter that John Hinckley wrote to Jodie Foster when he was in his hotel room after having seen President Reagan's itinerary, made his plan to go to the Hilton and then he sat down and wrote a letter to her addressed—[that is]—put her name on the envelope for the letter. This [was] not actually mailed, but he prepared it that morning, the morning of the 30th before going to the Hilton.

Q.   Without reading the letter, can you just summarize the substance of it?

A.   Yes. He says to her that he is going to assassinate President Reagan, that there is a definite possibility that he will be killed in his attempt to do that. He describes to her how he has tried to gain her attention and affection.... That time is running out on him. That he is not able to wait any longer to make her understand the importance of this and that he hopes in sacrificing his own life or his own freedom in what he refers to as an "historic deed" that he will finally gain her respect and love.

Q.   Is there a time written on that document, N–15?

A.   The date is 3/30/81, and the time is 12:45 p.m.

Q.   And shortly after that, Mr. Hinckley left for the Hilton Hotel?

A.   Yes.

Q.   And have you reviewed with Mr. Hinckley his thought processes that he was experiencing when he arrived at the Hilton Hotel up to and through the actual shooting?

A.   Yes, I have.

Q.   ... First, recite what you learned from Mr. Hinckley regarding his thought processes.

A.   Yes. Picking up then after he has prepared the letter, has loaded his weapon, he goes to the Hilton. What is on his mind is to see if he can in fact make an assassination attempt on Reagan; not knowing that that is possible, to decide whether or not to stay overnight again in Washington before going to New Haven or going on to New Haven then.

He is seeing two possible outcomes both now and in the immediate future, either the outcome of the assassination attempt and what happens to him in that process or, and what he assumes to be at least a termination of his freedom and a wish for termination of his life, and the other outcome being to proceed on to New Haven, which has been his primary plan during this period of time, to either kill himself or to kill Jodie Foster and himself. So those are the things that are on his mind.

When he arrives at the Hilton he said that he was surprised at how easy it was to get in the vicinity of where President Reagan would be. He had a sense there was something lapsed about the security, but was able to get in the vicinity, and when President Reagan arrived was fairly close to him as he went into the Hilton.

He said that, on his way in, ... President Reagan looked at him and smiled and waved and his own interpretation of that was something highly personal, that he felt that President Reagan was looking at him and smiling and waving.

President Reagan went on into the Hilton. John Hinckley left, left that location, walked up into the lobby of the Hilton and spent some time resting, trying to decide what to do.

He at that point assumed that President Reagan would be ... there for 45 minutes or an hour or so, some period of time, and he was debating whether to wait and see if he could get close to him as he departed, [or] whether he should go back to the hotel. There was still this issue about whether to go to New Haven, whether to stay overnight in Washington.

He walks back out of the hotel in what he estimates to be about 15 minutes later, goes back to the spot where he had been before and would have been, as he describes it, one or two minutes, but in a very quick period of time he is surprised that President Reagan's party is coming out again and as he comes out he has the experience of time moving very quickly, that is that there is only a moment before President Reagan [will] walk to his limousine and be out of the area, that he is there, is able to do it. [He] feels that President Reagan is about to turn again in his direction, and before the President has an opportunity to do that, he beings shooting.

Q. Doctor, how do you interpret Mr. Hinckley's mental state in those moments, those few moments before the actual shooting?

A. Well, his mental state is predominantly one of despair, depression, and a sense of the end of things. In terms of his own, as he can weigh and value things, the thing that is most important to him is to terminate his own existence and to find a way to do that. The suicidal aspects and self-destructiveness of this are foremost in his mind.

At the same time the wish for realization of this relationship with Jodie Foster is on his mind in terms of how his doing this act will unite him with Jodie Foster.

These are the primary things that are on his mind. There is a quickening of the time perspective at the moment that President Reagan is coming out and the sense of something highly personal in the encounter between the two.

... I can explain this by ... showing contrast and similarity to a previous experience. Remember that some months ago there had been a series of Jodie Foster films on TV in a short period of time, that he had sensed that they had been put there in some personal way in relationship to him, as a particular symptom or manifestation of illness that we see in some forms of illness. He had that same kind of highly personalized sense of when the President presumably waved and smiled to a crowd of people that he personalized on it and this [was] taking place in a very compacted time frame.

[A]s Mr. Hinckley described it, his experience of that opportunity for assassination was different from some earlier opportunities that he had had. He had been in situations on previous occasions where he could have shot at President-elect Reagan in early December and other high level officials when he was in town stalking. He feels that he was unable to act at those times in part because he would see them and there would be too long a period of time, whatever it would take to kind of provoke him into action, prompt action would take place, the timing of it was not sufficient. Some months before that he had tried to psych himself up when he was stalking President Carter because he wanted to make the act, but wasn't able to get himself to do it.

So that I think both the highly personalized quality in his experience and the rapid time frame became important and why this particular assassination attempt actually got taken to action while in earlier occasions when he had attempted to pull off some acts, he had been unable to act, but that was the mental state at the time.

Q. Doctor, you included in your description of his mental state [a] suicidal motive?

A. Yes, the primary, I mean his primary purpose in all of this is to terminate his own experience, his own existence so that is the predominant mental motivation that he is experiencing.

Cross Examination by Assistant U.S. Attorney Roger Adelman

Q. You have heard, have you not, the tapes of Mr. Hinckley talking to Jodie Foster; right?

A. Yes.

Q. Now, Mr. Hinckley told you that he went up there because he admired Miss Foster, he was interested in her; right?

A. Well, those two things are true. That doesn't quite capture what was on his mind about Miss Foster, but it is true that part of what was on his mind included admiration and an interest.

Q. Right. And he was in a way obsessed with her?

A. He was more than obsessed. I mean he was obsessed with her.

Q. Was he delusional about her?

A. Yes; he had developed delusional expectations of that relationship by that time.

Q. Now wait a minute. Are you telling this jury then that when Mr. Hinckley was up there on the telephone with Miss Foster and her roommates, that he was delusional?

A. He had delusions at that time, yes.

Q. What delusion did he have during the telephone calls that this jury heard? Name those delusions for us, please.

A. Oh, the whole, the basis of being there, including making the telephone calls, was based on delusional formation that he had in relationship to Jodie Foster....

He, by then, had come to believe that the only salvation that he had, the only way he could extricate himself from this life was through union with her.

He had come to believe that a union with her was in some sense ordained, that he was being propelled in that direction. He had taken it as a message to him that a number of her films had been shown on television during the time prior to that as the purpose—the purpose of that was a personal purpose, to spur him onward to activity in this regard.

He believed if he could make contact with her, that they could become an extraordinary couple.

He believed that he had some responsibilities toward her in terms of protecting her.

He believed that he could be made whole again in some sense in terms of the wretched existence and experiences that he was having.

[All] of these things ... are called a delusion because there are many components of false belief, and they are false beliefs that could not be readily shaken by evidence to the contrary, and they are beliefs upon which he is basing his activity, his plans, his actions.

In pursuing them he then makes telephone calls, and the delusions that are present during that whole period of time, including the telephone calls, are the type of thing I am saying.

This type of delusional formation would not [be expected] to interfere with ordinary activities like purchasing tickets or purchasing food or being able to make telephone calls.

There is considerable evidence that he did not have the kind of incoherence of thinking, the scattering of thoughts ... that can be an aspect of schizophrenia, and lead in certain periods of time during a person's life to much more incoherent activity. Those have never been present, to my knowledge, in John Hinckley....

The delusional formation—and of course this is very common to process schizophrenia—people can have long-term delusional formations at the same time they can be going to work everyday. They can be conducting their life outside of hospitals. They can be looking after families. So it is not an incompatibility with many areas of functioning that appears ordinary and accomplishes ordinary tasks, but the whole basis for [his] being there and making the telephone calls is [his] delusions....

Q. What you are saying is that nobody, including you, has ever found any observable delusions in this person, Mr. Hinckley; right?

A. Say that again.

Q. You are telling us in that long response there that nobody observed active delusions in Mr. Hinckley, right? Or manifestations?

A. A delusion is a mental process and it is not possible to have direct access to observe it....

You learn about delusions from learning about the person, what their beliefs are, and then by trying to see whether or not there are behaviors and impacts and effects on the person's life that are consistent with those beliefs.

Q. In other words—

A. So you can no more see a delusion than you can see whether or not someone believes in God.

I mean it is not there to be visualized as physical evidence, but it is there to be understood in a broad context with many derivative behaviors that would be compatible if its presence is claimed.

It is not based on simple reporting of something, but trying to determine in the overall flow of the person's life whether there are many derivative evidences that would be compatible with that conclusion.

Q. You are not telling this jury that there are not delusions that are readily observable by everyday people, are you? You are not telling them that generally?

A. The delusion, itself is a thought, a belief.

Q. If a man walks around—

A. You know that, you can know the presence of some delusions by observing.

For example, if a person has the delusion that they should take off their clothes and walk down the street, you can observe them walking down the street naked.

You cannot tell from that observation whether or not they, in fact, had that delusion. You cannot tell. It could be for some other reason, so the delusion is a belief system as I have defined it.

. . .

Q. . . . Now you mentioned in your testimony [that] Mr. Hinckley, as part of this delusional system at the time of the shooting, had an idea of reference about Mr. Reagan, that Mr. Reagan was waving at him, just him alone; is that right?

A. Yes, he personalized that experience and that would be an example of an idea of reference.

Q. You have examined and have read the report of the government doctors, that is to say, Drs. Cavanaugh, Dietz, and Rappeport, have you not?

A. Yes.

[The witness is shown a portion of the report summarizing statements by the defendant.]

Q. [Reading:] "He said that although he felt the President had looked right at him, he did not feel any message other than 'hello' was being communicated. He added: 'I was probably the only one he could see, so that is probably why he picked me out.' " Did you see that passage in this report before you testified today?

A. Yes.

Q. Mr. Hinckley reports to these doctors that there was no idea of reference at all, he just saw the President wave at him; right?

A. He thinks that the President has picked him out and I don't know that there is any evidence that President Reagan had singled him out.

Q. But he pointed out in the next sentence: "I was probably the only one he could see"; so that is probably why he picked him out.

A. That seems to me unlikely, that of the people there the only person he could see was John Hinckley, and in his description of the events to me, it was my inference that it was a highly personalized experience. This is a phenomen[on] that he has experienced on a number of other occasions, so it has some compatibility with the longitudinal view, and it is strange to me to think the only person President Reagan could see would be John Hinckley, and ... it strains my credulity to think President Reagan singled out John Hinckley and smiled and said hello to him personally.

Dr. Park Elliott Dietz, Government Witness

Direct Examination by Mr. Adelman

Q. ... Was there in the course of Mr. Hinckley's recitation of the events discussion or reference to the phenomenon of Mr. Reagan looking at him?

A. Yes, there was.

Q. All right. Now are you prepared to discuss the significance or lack thereof of that incident with respect to Mr. Hinckley's mental condition?

A. Yes, I am.

Q. All right, could you tell us about that, please?

A. Let me first mention that there is a symptom of some psychiatric disorders called "an idea of reference." And an idea of reference is a belief that something in the outside world has personal meaning for one.

And, of course, during a psychiatric evaluation, we are always looking for symptoms that could be part of a mental disorder, and there are certain kinds of things that a patient or a defendant may describe that leads one to think: "I wonder whether this is an idea of reference or not."

Now Mr. Hinckley did describe something for which I felt it was important to determine whether it was an idea of reference or not, and that was his description of the President having looked at him when the President arrived at the Hilton Hotel on March 30.

Q. Did you determine whether that was an idea of reference?

A. I believe I have, yes.

Q. What did you determine?

A. That it was not an idea of reference.

Q. How did you determine that?

A. Through Mr. Hinckley's own statements.

Q. What were they?

A. ... On June 7, 1981, in exploring possible evidence of ideas of reference, I asked Mr. Hinckley specifically about what he thought was happening when the President looked at him, and he said that he did not feel that any message other than "hello" was being communicated. He said he "was probably the only one he could see, so that is probably why he picked me out."

Q. What does that show you?

A. Well, had this been an example of an idea of reference or delusion[al] thinking, I believe that Mr. Hinckley would have said that the President meant to convey something to him personally, or that the President meant in some way to communicate "now was the time," or the President had some message to convey, or that this was "meant for him." None of those things were said.

He said that he believed the President meant to communicate "hello," and probably he was the only one that the President could see, which I took to [reflect] the fact that most of the other people there were cameramen who had cameras in front of their faces, so John Hinckley's face would be one of the few faces visible at the time.

Q. All right.

A. Also on June 7, 1981, I made note of another comment that Mr. Hinckley had made about the same incident in which he said, "He waved across the street and then waved to us, meaning other people where I was, and to cameramen and all, and then they rushed him inside, and when he waved to us I felt he was looking right at me, and I waved back. I was kind of startled but maybe it was just my imagination."

Q. Was that an idea of reference?

A. That was a statement that led me to inquire further about it. Hi[s] saying "Maybe it was just my imagination" leaves doubt.

Q. When you explored, what did you find and what did you conclude?

A. I found that he thought probably the President couldn't see anybody else and didn't intend to communicate anything other than "hello."

I would point out one other thing, and that is that these comments about the President waving are things that [were said] in June of 1981. There is an earlier account, as I've mentioned before, of the events of March 30, and that is the account in the file at Butner.[e] Dr. Johnson talked to Mr. Hinckley on April 3, just a few days after March 30, and got an account of the events of March 30, and the relevant quotation from that period reads as follows: "President got out and waved. John waved back."

Q. What is the significance of that?

A. Well, that says nothing that would even suggest an idea of reference.

Q. Do you draw any conclusions from the fact that 2½ months later he told you about the special significance of the waving?

A. Well, in order to draw conclusions from that I have to make inferences, and so far I've tried to keep my testimony to the facts and not to inference.

Q. Are there a number of inferences that can be made from that?

A. Yes, I think there are.

Q. Is manipulation one of the inferences, one of the many that could be made from this incident?

A. That is one of the possibilities.

Q. Was there discussion in your evaluation of Mr. Hinckley and, indeed, in his discussion of March 30 about the President looking at him when he exited the hotel?

A. Yes.

Q. All right. Now, could you evaluate that?

A. Yes. I think that the clearest statement on that was from an interview of July 12, 1981. This concerns when the President came out from the Hilton Hotel just prior to the shooting. What Mr. Hinckley said about that was: "I remember seeing Reagan. I remember seeing him wave to the people across the street and start to turn. I could see him flinch at the shots."

Q. Is that an idea of reference?

---

[e] Butner is the federal prison where Hinckley was detained before trial. Dr. Sally Johnson was the psychiatrist at Butner who evaluated Hinckley for the prosecution independently of Dr. Dietz and who also testified for the prosecution at the trial. [Footnote by eds.]

A.   It doesn't even suggest anything about personal communication or personal interpretation. [H]e saw [the President] wave to the people across the street and, indeed, that is what occurred.

Q.   If somebody interpreted that in this Court as an idea of reference, would that be an accurate interpretation?

A.   No, it would not.

. . .

Q.   Can you determine from all of your evaluation of the case, including interviews of Mr. Hinckley, as to whether, in fact, he had a delusion as to Miss Foster?

A.   I made such a determination.

Q.   What did you determine?

A.   That he has not had a delusion about Jodie Foster.

Q.   Now why do you have that view?

A.   From talking to him about it. You see, my first thought when I heard about this case prior to being personally involved, just based on media accounts, was that this sounded like a case that I happened to be particularly interested in, a type of case in which individuals do have a delusion of a relationship that isn't true. In fact, I had conducted a library search on that topic before getting any of the materials on the case just out of interest, because from the media accounts one would have thought that that is what this was about, that Hinckley would have had a delusional belief about Jodie Foster.

In talking to him, in learning the facts and learning about his actions and what else went on, it became clear that there is no delusion about Jodie Foster and there was no delusion about Jodie Foster. He recognized throughout that the relationship was one-sided—his care for her, his love for her—but that it was not reciprocated and that it was not likely to be reciprocated.

Q.   All right. This might be a useful time to turn to that matter of Jodie Foster, if we can.

THE COURT: Are you saying that in the absence of a return of interest there is no delusional pattern as far as he is concerned?

THE WITNESS: Well, there are other kinds of delusions, Your Honor, but delusional relationships in which a person has the delusion of a love relationship with someone else have to be two ways. There has to be a view that the other person somehow shares the relationship.

THE COURT: Could you give an example of that?

THE WITNESS: Surely. The young woman who is in love with a movie star from Hollywood and believes that every time a plane flies overhead it is his sending her a message of love. She writes him fan mail and then she gets answers because a plane flies over and she thinks it means he is saying, "Yes, I love you. Thank you for your letter."

These cases are reported with some frequency in the literature. We see it in both women and men—the delusion of relationship with another individual. For example, cases I have seen, Your Honor, include a young man who had the delusion that a particular woman might like him, loved him, and that he loved her. Now he may have loved her, but she didn't even know who he was. One day he broke into her apartment and ransacked the place, tore it apart and told me later he did that because he thought that she was being held hostage there. Well, that fellow is fine in every other area of his life, but he had a true delusion about his relationship with this woman, and she didn't even know him.

I have seen a variety of these cases, Your Honor.

BY MR. ADELMAN:

Q. Now could you compare that description you gave to the Court with Mr. Hinckley with respect to whether or not in your view he had a delusion as to Miss Foster?

A. In my opinion he did not have a delusion about Miss Foster.

Q. What is the reason or reasons that you say that? What is the evidence?

A. Well, let me tell you the evidence.

First of all, the development of his interest in Miss Foster took a perfectly natural course. He had seen her in movies. He saw her on television. He saw more of her movies. He became interested in her through that medium, and this is the first time he had become interested that way in a movie star. There was nothing special about the way he regarded seeing her in the movies. It is just that he was attracted to her and thought she would be a good person.

When he narrates his efforts to contact Jodie Foster by telephone, Mr. Hinckley has consistently narrated them to me in a manner indicating he understood that she was not really available to him. For example, in the very first interview we had with him, this is on May 30th, he said he felt that part of his fascination with Jodie Foster is that she was unattainable, out of reach, unapproachable.

He speculated that he knew all along that it wasn't going to work out, and that even when he went to New Haven, intending to introduce himself to her, he knew it wouldn't work.

Q. Why does that show it was not a delusion in your opinion?

A. Well, part of what would make this kind of belief system a delusion—and it is not even a belief system—what would render these ideas delusional would be a fixed false belief.

Q. Did he have a fixed false belief?

A. No, he didn't have a fixed belief, and it is hard to find evidence that he had a false belief. He had unrealistic hopes.

Q. What is that called besides—

A. That is called being a dreamer.

Q. Is being a dreamer a manifestation of serious mental disorder?

A. No, it isn't.

Q. Can you continue to tell us the evidence that you pointed to regarding the question whether this young lady, Miss Foster, was a delusion for Mr. Hinckley?

A. I will give you another example of what he said. He said, "She probably doesn't know what to make of me. I am probably just an aberration to her, but you know, she is getting a lot of publicity out of this and she is an actress and not exactly publicity shy. I am probably the best thing that ever happened to her career."

Q. How does that show he didn't have a delusional view of her?

A. Well, this is a rationalization after the fact, one way or the other, and I think that idea was actually an imitation of something Dr. Carpenter suggested to him. I think Dr. Carpenter's notes earlier than that date indicate that this was something he had suggested to Mr. Hinckley.

Q. What else do you have there regarding the question of delusions or not with regard to Jodie Foster?

A. In the first interview, Mr. Hinckley said that he had been—this is the first interview at which I was present—that he had been at Jodie Foster's door, but that he didn't knock or make an effort to introduce himself in person, and when asked why he hadn't, he said: "just basically shyness and insecurity. I mean, she was a pretty famous movie star and there I was, Mr. Insignificant himself."

Q. What does that show with respect to whether or not he had a delusion?

A. Well, it shows that he understood the reality of the situation, that she was a movie star and he wasn't.

Q. Before we go on, have you listened to the tape of Mr. Hinckley calling Miss Foster and at times her roommates that was recorded in September, 1980?

A. Yes, I have.

Q. Can you tell us whether in your view, Mr. Hinckley during that tape recording was delusional?

A. No, there is—

MR. FULLER: Object, Your Honor. Let the witness characterize his observations; I believe it would be appropriate.

THE COURT: All right. Handle it that way, Doctor.

How do you view that? How do you view that particular situation, that episode?

THE WITNESS: I think that the tape-recorded conversation with Jodie Foster and the tape-recorded conversation with her roommates indicate that Mr. Hinckley was indeed trying to make contact. I think it is notable that he did so politely, that he recognized the social nuance of the situation. He understood that it was expecting a lot to hope that Jodie Foster was going to spend much time with him on the phone. He showed that he was grateful when she did take the time to talk to him briefly. He politely asked if he might call back. He understood her answer to mean that he could, and he tried again to call her when she said it would be all right.

I think he was very sensitive to the social relationship and understood that here he was—a stranger—calling a woman who gets lots of these phone calls and who was of a very high status, and he understood his place in trying to contact her.

In addition, there is one other significant feature, I think, on those tapes, and that is the fact that, indeed, Jodie Foster says something to him about the roommates laughing at him. He hears laughter in the background, and he says, "What are they laughing at?" And she says, "They are laughing at you," and I think that that is probably the source of the statement in the Jodie letter that people at the dormitory are ridiculing him.

THE COURT: Is there anything else to be drawn from it?

THE WITNESS: From the tape?

THE COURT: From that conversation.

THE WITNESS: Well, the tape, Your Honor, I think shows an intact young man, a bit shy, but there is certainly no evidence of psychosis or delusional thinking in that tape.

THE COURT: All right.

. . .

Q. Doctor, let me show you Defense Exhibit Q–11 in evidence, a poem. . . . Now, does this in any way relate to Mr. Hinckley's view of Miss Foster?

A. Yes, it does.

Q. Basically and briefly could you tell us how?

A. This poem indicates an awareness that the relationship is one-sided, that he cannot expect anything from her, and I think the final verse says it all. It says, "Even a phone conversation seems to be asking too much, but I really can't blame you for ignoring a little twirp [sic] like me."

Q.   Does that suggest a delusion?

THE COURT: What does that suggest, if anything?

THE WITNESS: It suggests, points out the symptom that he is feeling bad about himself, regarding himself as "a little twirp." But the importance in this context is that it expresses an awareness that he cannot expect anything of Jodie Foster. This is what we call reality testing, the recognition that thinking that she is going to respond to him, an anonymous, or, rather, a stranger calling on the phone, is not realistic, and he recognizes that.

. . .

Q.   ... Did you learn in the course of your evaluation of Mr. Hinckley's goals for that day?

A.   Yes, I did.

Q.   Can you tell us what they were and what significance each of them has as far as your evaluation of his criminal responsibility is concerned?

A.   [D]uring the first interview that I had occasion to speak to Mr. Hinckley personally, ... Mr. Hinckley was asked if he had thought that after he carried out his plan of assassination, that Jodie Foster would know about him, and his response on that date was to smile and to say "Yeah, it worked."

Q.   Now, have you explored that with him either then or [in] other interviews?

A.   Yes. I will give you other examples of exploring that question.

On June 7, 1981, I interviewed Mr. Hinckley, and I asked him if he had been trying to impress Jodie Foster, and he said, "Well, it is a combination of things: To impress her, almost to traumatize her. That is the best word. To link myself with her for almost the rest of history, if you want to go that far."

I asked how he thought Jodie Foster would view him. He said, "I would have preferred for her to feel good about me, but going this way it is kind of hard for her to feel good about me."

I then asked him if he had been trying to communicate something to Jodie Foster, and he said that he had been trying to communicate something to the effect of, "Now you will appreciate how much I cared for you. I went to this extent. Now do you appreciate it?" ... I asked a follow-up to that, which was whether he thought he had accomplished that goal, and he said, "You know, actually, I accomplished everything I was going for there. Actually I should feel good that I accomplished everything on a grand scale." I asked him if he really meant that because that statement struck me as an extraordinary one, and he said, "Actually, I accomplished exactly what I wanted to accomplish, without exception."

Q. Now, with that as a goal or a series of goals, could you explain the significance of that [to] your evaluation of Mr. Hinckley and to whatever mental disorders you found that he has and to the general question of criminal responsibility. What does that mean in this case?

A. Well, from my general evaluation of Mr. Hinckley, what that statement means to me is that he did, indeed, intend to make an impression upon Jodie Foster; that he understood that the impression he would make ... with an act of this sort was a traumatic one, not likely to win affection, but one which would indeed impress upon her who he is and cause her to remember him; that he undertook the shootings of March 30 with [that] as a goal he had in mind. I believe there were other goals, but that is one he has articulated in writing, and that he believes he accomplished that goal which shows that his goal was indeed reasonable since he accomplished it.

Q. Does it show he was schizophrenic?

A. No, it doesn't.

Q. ... Does the fact that he had this particular goal show he suffered from a particular mental disorder?

A. That fact does not show that, no.

Q. Explain that to the jury.

A. Well, this goal certainly seems like a very odd one, and when I first heard that that was the goal—prior to my involvement in this case—I was impressed with what an odd and, in the lay sense, "crazy" thing such a goal would be.

After having the opportunity to evaluate Mr. Hinckley, to interview all of these other people, to review all of the facts, that goal makes sense. He had felt rejected by Jodie Foster as early as September, after his first efforts to contact her, and, as he later described, he was angry about what she had done, that is, that she had not responded to his calls as he hoped. To win her attention, to be able to impress upon her, here is John Hinckley who loves her, to make her remember him, was a goal for which he was willing to sacrifice a great deal. But it was not entirely a sacrifice, as I will show, because in addition to winning her attention, he wished to have fame and notoriety.

Q. Is that a separate goal?

A. Well, they are linked in this way, but it is a goal that I will show separate evidence for.

Q. All right. Do you have anything more to say about the goal insofar as it relates to a serious mental disorder?

A. Only to say that my first impression without the facts was that that could well reflect a serious mental disorder.

Q. Where do you stand today?

A. That it does not.

Q. Why?

A. Because I have had the opportunity to obtain the facts, to speak with him, and to determine that indeed that was a goal that developed out of his experiences in life and which he feels he has accomplished. . . .

Q. You mentioned the goal of—I believe it is—fame?

A. He displayed a considerable concern with the media, as I will show [a]nd he indicated his interest in assassination through not only the things I have referred to already, but comparisons he made between himself and other assassins.

Q. Does the fact he had the goal or purpose or whatever of fame show that he had a serious mental disorder?

A. No, the goal of becoming famous is not limited to those who are mentally disordered. In Mr. Hinckley's case, it does relate to [the] narcissistic personality disorder that I have diagnosed.

Q. Briefly, why is that?

A. That is because with narcissistic personality disorders, the view of one's self as special and more important than others may translate itself into a concern with becoming both the center of attention and famous to the extent of wanting to be in the media, wanting to be in history books. . . .

Cross Examination by Mr. Fuller

Q. You . . . discussed yesterday, doctor, a motive on Mr. Hinckley's part that you described as a desire for fame, is that correct?

A. That is correct.

Q. And I believe you described that as being a quality of a narcissistic personality disorder?

A. Well, to be precise about it, the quality of narcissistic personality disorder includes a preoccupation with fantasies of unlimited success and fame and other kinds of glory.

Q. But what I am saying is the idea of desiring fame, you have put into the cluster of features that go to make up a narcissistic personality disorder, is that correct?

A. Well, I didn't put it there. It is there as one of the listed diagnostic features. Of course there are people interested in fame who don't suffer from any disorder at all, but in this instance I think the desire for fame is related to that disorder.

Q. I didn't mean to imply that you wrote DSM–III and put that particular characteristic under the heading "Narcissistic Personality Disorder." But I do mean to ask, is it not so that you have identified that feature as one which you observed in Mr. Hinckley as supporting your diagnosis of his suffering from a narcissistic personality disorder?

A. Yes, it is. Of course it is also the case that part of his concern with fame may have nothing to do with personality disorder. It is hard to know how much of that concern comes from this personality feature and how much of it is independent of it.

Q. And is it fair to characterize this idea of fame [as] an idea of grandiosity?

A. Well, it is a grandiose concern and a grandiose preoccupation if one continues it to the point of fantasizing unlimited success, unlimited fame, and so on. It is not a grandiose delusion, which is another matter altogether.

Q. If it were a grandiose delusion, it then, of course, would it not, become a personality feature associated with the disease of schizophrenia?

A. Yes. Well, yes. Grandiose delusions are often found in schizophrenia as well as in other disorders, and that is when a person believes that they already are successful or famous or has a delusion—of being Napoleon or Jesus Christ—examples of grandiose delusions.

Q. Well, there are other grandiose delusions short of thinking you are Napoleon, are there not?

A. Yes, there are.

Q. ... There is quite an array of the delusions that might go into delusions of grandiosity?

A. Yes, indeed. I have heard many of them.

.   .   .

Q. ... Yesterday we were discussing referential thinking, and I alluded to the occasion on March 30 when the President entered the Hilton Hotel and waved in the direction of Mr. Hinckley. Do you recall that?

A. Yes, I do.

Q. And you expressed your opinion that was not referential thinking?

A. That is correct.

Q. Now, is it not correct, sir, that in direct examination you told us that you had learned from the defendant that "... the President meant to communicate 'hello' and probably he," the defendant, "was the only one the President could see. Which I took to mean the fact that most of the other people there were cameramen who had cameras in front of their faces, so John Hinckley's face would be one of the few faces visible at the time." Do you recall that?

A.   I recall that, and that is one of the things Mr. Hinckley told me, and that is what I took it to mean when he told me that.

Q.   ... I'm going to ask you to look at Government's Exhibit 22 in evidence, Dr. Dietz, and ask if that is a photograph which purports to represent that moment in time just shortly before or shortly after the President had arrived at the Hilton on March 30, 1981?

A.   My understanding is that this photograph was taken at approximately 1:45 p.m. and that this is prior to the President's arrival at the Hilton Hotel. He did not arrive at 1:45 is my understanding.

Q.   I'm saying it is the only photograph we have in which Mr. Hinckley is depicted prior to the arrival of the President?

A.   Yes, that is right.

Q.   And, looking at that photograph, is Mr. Hinckley the only person that could be seen by one moving from the limousine to the entrance of the Hilton?

A.   When this was taken the cameramen did not have the cameras in front of them because the President hadn't arrived, so, of course, there are many faces visible.

(iii) Hinckley's Capacity to Appreciate Wrongfulness. Each of the testifying experts was asked to express an opinion on the "ultimate" issues before the jury—i.e. whether, as a result of mental disease, the defendant lacked substantial capacity to appreciate the wrongfulness of his conduct or to conform his conduct to the requirements of the law. None of the experts declined to express such an opinion. As might be expected, the defense experts concluded that Hinckley lacked the requisite capacity while the prosecution experts reached the opposite conclusion. This and the following sections present excerpts from the expert testimony on the "appreciation" and "control" issues.

Before the "appreciation" testimony is read, the discussion on the meaning of "know" and "wrong" at pages 12–14, above, should be consulted. The issues described there were raised in a pretrial "motion hearing" in the *Hinckley* case, at which the parties requested a ruling by the trial judge on the meaning of "appreciation." The prosecution contended that the term should be construed to encompass only "cognitive" factors and to exclude "emotional" or "affective" impairment. In its argument, the government noted that the decision adopting the Model Penal Code insanity test in the District of Columbia, *United States v. Brawner*, was silent on the meaning of "appreciate," and that the court therefore should consider the intentions of the drafters of the Model Penal Code. According to the government's interpretation, the

Model Code drafters intended to carry forward the traditional *M'Naghten* inquiry under the "appreciation" prong while encompassing emotional and volitional incapacities under the "control" prong of the test. The government also pointed out that most of the leading federal appellate opinions referred to the appreciation criterion as the "cognitive" prong of the test, thus implying that it referred to a narrow meaning of "know" and "wrong."

The defense argued, to the contrary, that the *Brawner* court intended "to depart from the narrow, constricted view of knowledge as used in the historical *M'Naghten* test" and meant to adopt a "forward-looking, modern view" of appreciation. Appreciation, the defense contended, requires a "degree of understanding far beyond that mere ability to verbalize that [a] particular act is wrong," and encompasses affective factors as well as cognitive ones. The defense proposed an instruction to this effect: "appreciation refers not only to a verbal cognizance or simple awareness of the wrongfulness of his actions, but to an affective or emotional understanding of his conduct as well."

During the course of the argument, the trial court asked whether the government would object to an instruction defining appreciation to mean "not only a verbal cognizance or simple awareness of the wrongfulness of one's conduct, but also an awareness and understanding of the import and consequences of one's behavior."

The government responded as follows:

An instruction along those lines would be more than adequate, if, during the testimony the psychiatrists know what the proper standard is. [Otherwise] what will happen in this case is that ... every defense psychiatrist is going to get up and say that emotional appreciation is part of this test and they will speak to whether or not John Hinckley could [emotionally] appreciate the wrongfulness of his acts. If all the jury is told in the end, in that circumstance, is to [consider] whether or not he could 'appreciate the wrongfulness of his acts,' obviously what they will consider is whether he could [emotionally appreciate] the wrongfulness of his acts as well, and this will have effected a reconstitution of the standard.

Following this discussion, Judge Parker ruled as follows:

I will approach the word appreciation ... within the context of a cognitive definition. Now, at an appropriate time [during the trial], I'm going to set the guideline; ... when the testimony comes, I'll hear you as to a particular piece of testimony and evidence....

The Court also indicated that it had not yet "decided on any instruction" on this issue.

Dr. William T. Carpenter, Jr., Defense Witness

Direct Examination by Mr. Fuller

Q. Doctor, have you an opinion whether at the time of the shooting on March 30, 1981, the defendant, as a result of the mental disease you have described, lacked substantial capacity to appreciate the wrongfulness of his conduct?

A. Yes, I do have an opinion on that.

Q. Would you please express that opinion?

A. ... My opinion is that he did have a lack, substantial lack of capacity to appreciate the wrongfulness of his conduct on March 30.

The basis for that opinion is the following: I think the term "appreciate" has—I have tried to think about three elements that are relevant to a person's ability to appreciate wrongfulness, the first of which would be what I would term a cognitive or just a pure thinking type of understanding, and this understanding would be the sort of thing that one could get at if you give a true-false quiz at the time. If the question was: Do you know that shooting the President of the United States is illegal, and you answer that true or false and in that sense of just the pure knowledge unrelated to his reasoning about that knowledge or his emotional state, Mr. Hinckley did.

THE COURT: Come to the Bench, counsel.

(At the Bench:)

THE COURT: ... What is his answer going to be?

MR. FULLER: His answer, Your Honor, will be a mixture. You heard him say that he would pass a true-false test.

THE COURT: Well, he talks about—he says several factors. He expressed the [cognitive] factor.

MR. FULLER: ["Cognitive"] meaning only the veneer of being able to say to shoot somebody is wrong. He will go beyond that, he will go into the question of Mr. Hinckley's reasoning abilities, his ability to appreciate the terms of his reasoning powers, the impairment of the reasoning processes which, I believe, Your Honor, is clearly embraced within the term "appreciate" as used in *Brawner*, as I think the Government has conceded in some of its papers.

MR. ADELMAN: Your Honor, our concern is that this man typically is confused. ... Might I point out that [in] his report [he] indicated that ... "Mr. Hinckley retained an intellectual appreciation of wrongfulness," and added, "In my judgment, the emotional component, as in so much of his life, was preeminent at the time of the crime." ... Elsewhere in his conclusions he indicates that though Mr. Hinckley had cognitive appreciation he lacked the emotional appreciation.

Now, Your Honor ruled [at the pretrial hearing] that . . . appreciation is limited to cognition. . . .

My only concern here is that the doctor, who obviously doesn't know
the law like we do, be instructed that he should testify in terms of
cognition. Based on his report and based on the manner in which he
testifies, it appears he was about to talk about volition and emotion and
things of that character.

Your Honor has ruled that [out], though. I think the matter can be
swiftly dealt with if Your Honor would simply instruct him to talk about
cognition only.

That was the Court's ruling and I believe he can deal with that.

THE COURT: What is your thought?

MR. FULLER: Your Honor, he will testify that in cognition there is
an element of reason. You cannot compartmentalize the mind into rigid
compartments: This is cognition, and this is will, and this is emotion.

There is a whole list of approaches that must be taken of the term
"appreciate" and when you use the word "cognition" as it is used in
literature, [which] the Government cites, . . . there is included in cognition an element beyond the mere ability to verbalize that I know
something is right or I know something is wrong. . . . There is included
in the element of cognition, Your Honor, a quality of reason, and I expect
this witness to develop that aspect of the appreciation issue in terms of
what Mr. Hinckley did on March 30.

MR. ADELMAN: Whatever you say about Dr. Carpenter I think he
is an intelligent man, and I think he can follow a simple instruction from
this Court that appreciation is limited to cognition because otherwise he
is going to slip back into the area that Your Honor ruled out.

THE COURT: Well, Mr. Adelman, I don't want to put shackles on
this man to the extent that he can't advance his point of view as he says
the word appreciation and the concept of appreciation.

Of course, you see when this matter goes to the jury the Court is
going to give the instructions of law and the jury is bound by it. . . .

What this witness testifies to and what the jury will be bound by
insofar as questions of law and the instructions of law are concerned are
two different things. And I can indicate that—I can give it as a caution-
ary instruction as of now that the [expert witness] may, in discussing
these matters, advance notions which the Court does not recognize and
which will not be within the confines of the jury instructions. . . .

MR. FULLER: Your Honor, . . . I think what you have alluded to is
what you have already done in the *Washington*[f] instructions. It is what

---

[f] The reference is to Washington v. United States, 390 F.2d 444 (D.C.Cir.1967), in
which the court discussed the problems associated with "conclusory" expert testimo-

you are suggesting to be done now, that is to say, ultimately it is the Court's instructions that will govern the jury's deliberation. That is a very critical issue.

THE COURT: Mr. Adelman, what do you say?

MR. ADELMAN: [I]f the Court will instruct the jury that appreciation is limited to cognition, then to have this man testify that it is more than that is quite misleading and really undermines the Court instruction.

Now, we are not asking Dr. Carpenter to say one word less about anything he has to say, except that he should testify within the framework of what the law means by appreciate. If he can do that, fine, but to have him go on and talk about emotional appreciation, which is his theory maybe, he then invades the province of the Court. He becomes the definer of the law.

THE COURT: Well, I can make it clear tomorrow. I can make it clear to him. I don't want to be in a position of just cutting them off at the knees. However, I will indicate to them, Mr. Fuller, that the instructions—you are attempting to develop more out of the concept of appreciation in *Brawner* than what is in the four corners. You advance the notion that *Brawner* is an advanced approach to this whole field of psychiatry and the defense of insanity, and *Brawner* must be read within the liberal context that you view it and as others view it, but until the Court of Appeals or some authoritative source speaks and embraces and extends the concept to the extent that you want to extend it, I am not willing to do it. At the same time, I am not willing to just summarily cut your witness off.

I can indicate in no uncertain terms to the jurors that what they are to follow, that they may hear concepts, that the ultimate, that the ultimate ruling guidelines that they are to follow are given by the Court in the instructions of law. . . .

MR. ADELMAN: Your Honor, the point we wanted to make is that this will open up our experts to coming in and rebutting, if you will, the concept of emotional appreciation. In other words, we will create a new battleground.

THE COURT: Listen, you have the battleground in any event. You are going to have battlegrounds in any event. They are going to be at opposite ends of the poles as to this question of capacity.

MR. ADELMAN: The problem is, and I can see the Court's point, but the problem is we now have the experts defining a legal standard.

ny, including the risk of undue reliance by the jury on expert opinion concerning the "ultimate" issues in the case. The court appended to its opinion guidelines for jury instructions designed to emphasize the proper scope of the witness' expertise and the jury's ultimate responsibility to find the facts and apply the law. [Footnote by eds.]

If Your Honor feels it is suitable to tell the jury that, I would suggest this: It is our suggestion that Your Honor instruct this witness that appreciation is limited to cognition in the presence of the jury, and then go to inform the jury that they will be bound by the instructions of the Court and that the doctor may testify beyond the bounds of the law or the Court's instructions.

THE COURT: No. What I will do, I will indicate to them—what I will do in this instance is indicate to them that they will hear the doctors, they will hear [t]he experts. As I indicated in the *Washington* Instruction, undoubtedly they are going to hear wide extremes, or not wide extremes, but wide differences in the presentation of the psychiatrists; that the legal principles that will govern their [decision on] the question of insanity will be given by the Court and even though they may have references and thoughts [in] the testimony by the doctors which get into the area of the law, that they are to disregard it; that the ultimate instructions of law as they apply to the events are given by the Court.

MR. FULLER: We ultimately agree that Your Honor's instructions are . . . going to govern here, but we urge that this man is a psychiatrist, and he must be able to talk in his terms.

THE COURT: All right.

MR. FULLER: And I ask also, Your Honor, that no instruction be given before Dr. Carpenter resumes the stand and concludes his testimony. We will be finished in a matter of minutes and I would like, if you are going to give any instruction, it be done afterwards.

THE COURT: I will do it afterwards.

MR. ADELMAN: Your Honor indicated [at the pretrial hearing] that the appropriate time, when the testimony comes, you said you will hear us as to that and that is why we are here.

THE COURT: I understand that.

MR. ADELMAN: We are asking for an instruction.

THE COURT: I will give the instructions afterwards. That is the way I will handle it.

MR. ADELMAN: All right.

(In Open Court:)

THE COURT: Dr. Carpenter, return to the stand.

(Whereupon, the witness returned to the stand.)

THE COURT: Dr. Carpenter, are you aware of the *Brawner* instructions?

THE WITNESS: Yes.

THE COURT: And are you aware of the *Washington* instruction?

THE WITNESS: Yes.

THE COURT: Very well.

BY MR. FULLER:

Q.   I have to recall in my mind where we were.

Doctor, I believe I had asked you whether you had an opinion as to whether at the time of the shooting on March 30, 1981 the defendant, as a result of the mental disease you described, lacked the substantial capacity to appreciate the wrongfulness of his conduct.

THE COURT: I know he answered that.

BY MR. FULLER:

Q.   You answered that, I believe, that you had an opinion?

A.   Yes.

Q.   Would you please tell us what that opinion is?

A.   Yes, that I do think that he had—lacked substantial capacity to appreciate the wrongfulness of his conduct.

Q.   Would you in your own terms elaborate on that and explain to the jury what you mean when you say he "lacked capacity to appreciate the wrongfulness of his conduct"?

A.   Yes. In forming an opinion about his ability to appreciate wrongfulness, I tried to look at three components of that, the components in real life that are merged together, but found it useful to try to think of each separately.

The first was whether there was a purely intellectual understanding that what he did was illegal. And it is my opinion on a purely intellectual level that he didn't know that he had that knowledge, that those were illegal acts.[g]

The ability to reason that is implied in appreciation: I think appreciation of wrongfulness would mean that a person had an ability to reason about it, to think about it, to understand the consequences, to draw inferences about the acts and their meaning. And reasoning processes, which involve both the intellectual component and the emotional component. It is part of what goes together in our reasoning about any issue. That in this regard I believe Mr. Hinckley lacked substantial capacity to appreciate.

The reason for this opinion is that it is an understanding of the very reasoning process he was going through in preparation for and in carrying out the acts, that in his own mind, his own reasoning, the predominant reasoning had to do with two major things, the first of

[g] The witness either said or meant to say: "And it is my opinion [that] on a purely intellectual level that he did know, that he had that knowledge, that those were illegal acts." [Footnote by eds.]

which was the termination of his own existence; the second of which was to accomplish this union with Jodie Foster through death, after life, whatever. But these were the major things that were dominating his reasoning about it. The magnitude of importance to him in weighing and in his reasoning of accomplishing these aims was far greater than the magnitude of the events per se. And in that regard it was not only his mind. He was not able to—he was not reasoning about the legality issue itself.

On the more emotional side of appreciation, which would have to do with some—with the feelings, the emotional appreciation or understanding of the nature of the events, the consequences, he also had an impairment in that regard. And the impairment there was that the emotional consequences of the acts that he conducted were in his experience solely in terms of the inner world he had constructed. The meaning of this to the victims of the act was not on his mind. I don't mean to be crass about this, but in his mental state the effect of this on the President [and] on any other victims was trivial, that they—in his mental state they were bit players who were there in a way to help him to accomplish the two major roles [on] which his reasoning was taking place and were not in and of themselves important to this.

So that I do think that he had a purely intellectual appreciation that it was illegal. Emotionally he could give no weight to that because other factors weighed far heavier in his emotional appreciation.

And as these two things come together in his reasoning process, his reasoning processes were dominated by the inner state—by the inner drives that he was trying to accomplish in terms of the ending of his own life and in terms of the culminating relationship with Jodie Foster.

It was on that basis that I concluded that he did lack substantial capacity to appreciate the wrongfulness of his acts.

Q.   In considering his cognitive awareness, doctor, does that include an element of reason as well?

A.   ... You see, reason is where the purely emotional and purely cognitive parts don't take place independent of each other. They come together and that is around the reasoning.

The cognitive part, just for clarity of thinking about it, [consider an] analogy that might help explain what I am thinking about there. If one were in a medical emergency, rushing someone to the hospital and you asked the true/false question ... "Are you aware that the speed you are going is breaking the law?" There would be a cognitive appreciation, but in their reasoning around what they are doing, because of the emotional importance of what is going on, this cognitive appreciation would not be having a major impact on their reasoning about what they are doing.

So in my view the purely intellectual and purely emotional doesn't exist independent of each other, but they come together in the reasoning.

And it is the impact on his reasoning that I have tried to describe predominantly in understanding his impairment in his ability to appreciate wrongfulness.

MR. FULLER: I have no further questions, Your Honor.

Cross Examination by Mr. Adelman

Q. He made a decision not to shoot Mr. Carter [in Dayton on October 2]?

A. He made a decision to leave his gun behind, to go without the gun, to see if he could get more into the frame of mind by getting in the proximity of President Carter to do it.

Q. He made a decision to leave the gun at the hotel?

A. Yes.

Q. Because he knew it was wrong to carry a gun into the streets, particularly near the President of the United States?

A. He didn't leave it in the room because he was concerned with the wrongfulness of carrying it in the presence of the President.

Q. Can't you infer that he knew on that day that he knew that carrying a gun out on the streets of Dayton was wrong? Yes or no.

A. He in that purely intellectual sense has always known that carrying a gun like that was wrong, was illegal. But what I'm saying is it is not because of that consideration that he left the gun behind. He left the gun behind for other reasons, not because he was mindful. I don't think he was concerned with the legality of it one way or the other. He was concerned with other things he was trying to accomplish for himself and it met his needs at that point to go without the gun, trying to see how close he could [get]—and see if he could get himself into a different state of mind.

THE COURT: Namely what?

THE WITNESS: He wanted—he had on his mind . . . the despair he felt as he left New Haven and his inability to make a simple and successful encounter of Jodie Foster. He was now trying to get himself back into a frame of mind where he felt more competent, more able, more effective in life [and he] found himself doing this by taking on the Travis Bickle parallel.

He felt he could accomplish this—and he did have suicidal thoughts at the time—through the stalking of President Carter. In that context he then is trying to psych himself up to get the impulses more intense, trying to prompt himself to be able to take action on them, so that he had, if you will, the mental scenario in place.

There was not the intensive impulsivity that could lead to his taking action and he was doing things to increase the likelihood.

Q. That is your explanation for what he did and didn't do in Dayton?

A. Yes.

. . .

Q. Now he then went to Nashville the following week, right?

A. Yes.

Q. And you are aware that he traveled again by airplane to that city, correct?

A. Yes.

Q. And he checked in at a hotel near the Grand Old Opry where President Carter was due to give a speech on the 9th of October?

A. Yes.

Q. He was again stalking the President, right?

A. Yes.

Q. And he got himself into a position where he would be close to the President once more, correct?

A. Yes.

Q. And more particularly, he got himself into the airport complex where the President was passing through, right?

A. Well, yes, he was in there. Yes.

Q. So he was able to organize his behavior in that fashion to get himself within range of the President, right?

A. Yes.

Q. And on this occasion did he think he was Travis Bickle?

A. The same situation that I described before.

Q. Well, can you tell us, yes or no, did he think he was Travis Bickle?

A. He found himself living out parallels of Travis Bickle. He did not believe himself to be Travis Bickle.

Q. You are aware that he was arrested by the Nashville Airport Police that day and found to be in possession of several guns, right?

A. Yes.

Q. You are aware that the police processed him through their processing system, right?

A. Yes. Well, they got the guns as they were in a suitcase and the suitcase was being taken through by a porter.

Q. What I am asking you is are you aware that Mr. Hinckley gave information to the police upon arrest?

A.   Yes.

Q.   And he didn't say he was Travis Bickle when he was talking to the police, did he?

A.   No.

Q.   He told them that he was John W. Hinckley, Jr., correct?

A.   Correct.

Q.   On that occasion he took it upon himself to hide the weapons in the suitcase, right?

A.   Yes.

Q.   He didn't carry them openly about his person, did he?

A.   No.

Q.   And he knew, did he not, by that fact, by secreting the weapons, that the possession of weapons down there in Tennessee in public was wrong, right?

A.   Yes. Yes.

Q.   And he attempted to hide the weapons so that he wouldn't be detected?

A.   Right.

Q.   He appreciated the wrongfulness of that conduct, didn't he?

A.   He knew it was illegal to carry the weapons publicly.

Q.   Right. Furthermore, he told you on that occasion in his suitcase was a diary. Do you recall that testimony?

A.   Yes.

Q.   And he told you further that after being apprehended by the police, he destroyed the diary, is that correct?

A.   That is correct.

Q.   You have never seen the diary?

A.   I have not.

Q.   To your knowledge no one else has besides Mr. Hinckley?

A.   That's right. He said he tore it up and flushed it away, so no one would have seen that.

Q.   He claimed in the diary were indications of the stalking—

A.   He had kept a diary of the stalking behavior during that period of time, yes.

Q.   And the fact that he threw the diary away indicates that that was behavior that the police could determine to be wrong, right?

A.   Yes.

Q.   Therefore, he appreciated the wrongfulness of that?

A.   Therefore he knew that it was illegal. Appreciate, as I think I have tried to characterize it, as I understand it, in terms of the legal standard for crime responsibility is broader than just the intellectual knowledge. But he always knew that what he was doing with the guns—

THE COURT: Doctor, don't get into a discourse on that particular area.

THE WITNESS: He knew it was illegal.

Q.   Let's just establish [that] we will get to this later. Your discussion of appreciation yesterday was your medical view. You don't know what the law defines appreciation as, do you?

A.   What I am trying to indicate to you, when you use the word appreciate, that it has a broader connotation than what you were just asking, your question before, that as I understand the word appreciate to mean.

Q.   As you understand it it is a medical understanding, not a legal understanding, right?

A.   As I understand it it is, as a medical expert trying to apply that understanding to the legal standards that are at issue in these proceedings.

. . .

Q.   Now, having been arrested, Mr. Hinckley never revealed that arrest to his parents throughout the next months, did he?

A.   That is correct.

Q.   And he didn't tell Dr. Hopper?

A.   No.

Q.   And as far as we know, he didn't tell other family members as well, right?

A.   Correct.

Q.   And one of the reasons he didn't do that was that he didn't want them to know that he had done something wrong, right?

A.   Yes.

Q.   He had been, in other words, performing an illegal act and didn't want other people to know about it?

A.   That is correct.

Q.   And to that extent he was able to conform his behavior; that is, to keep that secret within him?

A.   Right.

Q.   Now likewise, Mr. Hinckley never told family members or Dr. Hopper about the stalking, correct?

A.   Correct.

Q.   Nor did he tell anybody else as far as we can tell, right?

A.   That's right.

Q.   And he didn't tell them—well, you would agree with me that the stalking behavior was wrong. It was illegal. It is not proper to stalk the President of the United States and try to hurt him?

A.   That's right.

Q.   And again Mr. Hinckley—one of the reasons Mr. Hinckley didn't do that was that he realized that what he had done was wrong and he didn't want those close to him to know that, right?

A.   Yes.

Q.   To put it another way, he knew that his behavior was wrong and he conformed his own inner workings not to reveal it. He kept it a secret, right?

A.   It was part of keeping an enormous number of things secret that went together, some of which were illegal.

Q.   All right. I want to talk about those if we can. Now after Nashville, you are aware that Mr. Hinckley in the month of October traveled to Texas, right?

A.   Yes.

Q.   And indeed he made another trip to New Haven, correct?

A.   Yes.

Q.   And then he went and purchased two more guns down in Texas on the 13th of October or thereabouts?

A.   Right.

Q.   Once more he didn't reveal that purchase of weapons to anybody, did he?

A.   No.

Q.   And he realized that it was wrong for him to be walking around, indeed flying around the country with weapons, correct?

A.   Yes.

Q.   And he did not reveal [that] to anybody because he knew that that was wrong and he didn't want people close to him to know?

A.   Well, there again it is just a bit more complicated. There was a lot that went together that he wasn't revealing and there were a number of reasons, not just the wrongness of those acts, upon which he based, holding it secret.

Q.   But the wrongness was part of it?

A.   Yes.

. . .

Q.   What was the planning that he undertook [before going to the Hilton on March 30]?

A.   The planning was to get dressed, load the gun and to get himself over to the Hilton.

Q.   I take it the planning also included wearing a jacket so that the gun wouldn't be seen. Would you add that to it?

A.   Yes. The gun was concealed, yes.

Q.   He did that because he knew it is illegal to carry a gun in Washington and he would be arrested if he were seen carrying it in his hand up the Hilton, right?

A.   Right.

Q.   And again he did that because he knew that the Secret Service, as other people, would know it is wrong for a man to come up and stand with a gun in his hand right at the President's side, right?

A.   He did it because he knew that if they saw him, they would interfere with what he was going to do and that he wouldn't achieve his aims.

Q.   True, but he also realized that it was wrong.

A.   Well, you are asking me why he did certain things and he did, he concealed the gun, concealed this so that there wouldn't be an interference of his carrying out his plan. He didn't—it was not utmost in his mind [that he didn't] want to be caught doing something illegal. What was uppermost in his mind was terminating his existence.

Q.   But whether it was uppermost or not, it was in his mind?

A.   The terminating of his existence was in his mind. He wasn't spending time thinking about whether this breaks the law or not. He was spending time pursuing his major goal at that point.

Q.   Well, whether it was a major goal or not a major goal, he knew that carrying a gun going to the Hilton and doing what he planned to do was wrong?

A.   He would have had that knowledge, yes.

Q.   And you would agree with me that from the time he had this thought of shooting the President until he did it, he did not reveal to anybody his intent . . .

A.   That is correct.

Q.   . . . except in that letter [to Jodie Foster]?

A.   Well, he wrote it in the letter, but this, of course, didn't get to anybody else.

Q. He was able then, in other words, to conceal his intent from the third parties who might interfere with his plan?

A. Yes, he was.

Dr. Park Elliott Dietz, Government Witness

Direct Examination by Mr. Adelman

Q. [L]et me ask you ... whether at the time of the criminal conduct on March 30, 1981, the defendant, as a result of mental disease or defect, lacked substantial capacity to appreciate the wrongfulness of his conduct?

A. I ... made a determination on that point.

Q. What is that determination?

A. That determination is that on March 30, 1981, Mr. Hinckley, as a result of mental disease or defect, did not lack substantial capacity to appreciate the wrongfulness of his conduct.

. . .

Q. Can you tell us [t]he evidence that you have evaluated and set forth that indicates that Mr. Hinckley was on that day able to appreciate the wrongfulness of his conduct?

A. The answer is yes, I can provide some of the evidence. I will summarize. I will need to summarize a bit to do that because I have already presented some of the evidence to that effect.

Let me begin by saying that the evidence of Mr. Hinckley's ability to appreciate wrongfulness on March 30, 1981 has a background. That background includes long-standing interest in fame and assassinations. It includes study of the publicity associated with various crimes. It includes extensive study of assassinations. It includes choice of Travis Bickle as a major role model, a subject I will tell you about when I describe "Taxi Driver." It includes his choice of concealable handguns for his assassination plans, and his recognition that the 6.5 rifle he purchased was too powerful for him to handle. It includes his purchase of Devastator exploding ammunition on June 18, 1980. It includes multiple writings about assassination plans.

Q. Continue.

A. Now on that backdrop we see specific behaviors involved in Mr. Hinckley's pursuit of the President. His purchase of guns in Lubbock, Texas, in September of 1980 may or may not have been made after a decision to stalk President Carter. I say "may or may not" because there is a late-coming piece of evidence to the effect that Mr. Hinckley may have considered or actually stalked President Carter in March of 1980. He never mentioned that to me. He never mentioned that to my colleagues. I believe he mentioned that very recently to Dr. Goldman, as recently as during the trial.

Laying that aside, since I have no way to determine if that is true that he stalked or considered stalking in March of 1980, I know that he had made the decision by the time that he went to—that he left Lubbock, Texas, for Dayton, Ohio, to stalk and shoot President Carter. We can tell you more about that stalking, but his stalking of President Carter in Dayton for which he tried to "psych himself up," as he put it, and stalking of President Carter in Nashville when he tried to "psych himself up," as he put it, are all part of the backdrop—are all part of the evidence that goes to show he understood on March 30th what assassination was, how it was carried out, and the consequences of assassination, which he knew from his study of the subject.

When he traveled to Dallas to purchase guns in October '80 after his arrest in Nashville, he was replacing his arsenal, which had been confiscated by the police there. He made the decision to switch his target from President Carter to President-elect Reagan after the November 4, 1980, election. He concealed successfully all of his stalking from his parents, from his brother, from his sister, from his brother-in-law, and from Dr. Hopper, including hiding his weapons, hiding his ammunition, and misleading them about his travels and his plans. This concealment indicates that he appreciated the wrongfulness of his plans, of his stalking behavior, throughout that entire time period and is further evidence of his appreciation of the wrongfulness on March 30, 1981.

Mind you, no single piece of evidence is determinative here. I am providing you with examples of kinds of evidence that, taken together, make up an opinion about his appreciation of wrongfulness on March 30th, and these are examples of some of those pieces of evidence.

He purchased a highly concealable, .38 caliber revolver the day after Reagan's inauguration. He indicated that he became interested in President Reagan's whereabouts in March of 1981 before he had even begun his trip to Washington, D.C. He said he had become interested in the President's whereabouts.

When we get closer to the events of March 30th his decision on that day to, as he put it, "check out the scene" and to see how close he could get at the Hilton Hotel indicates that his decision to go to the Hilton Hotel reflected his thoughts about committing assassination on that day. He wanted to know how close he could get. Could he get within range? Could he get a clear shot?

He wrote a letter, having made his decision, to Jodie Foster, and we discussed that today already. In that letter to Jodie Foster, he indicated he was going to attempt to get Reagan and he indicates his knowledge that he could be killed by the Secret Service in the attempt. That is an indication that he understood and appreciated the wrongfulness of his plans because the Secret Service might well shoot someone who attempted to kill the President.

His decision to load his revolver with exploding ammunition before he left room 312 at the Park Central Hotel: Again, decisionmaking reflecting a choice of the use of explodable bullets which would have maximum effect on the victim, and understanding of the wrongfulness of his behavior, and understanding of the damage that he might bring upon other people.

His concealment of his revolver in his right pocket because he shoots right-handed: A decision to have his revolver where he could quickly draw it and understanding that the purpose of taking the revolver with him was to shoot.

His waiting until he had a clear shot at the President before drawing his gun: He didn't draw his gun when the President first arrived at the Hilton Hotel, as I have indicated before, because he didn't have a clear shot when the presidential motorcade first arrived. The limousine was farther away, and there was a curve in the wall between Mr. Hinckley and where the President entered the building. His waiting until the President came within his accurate range before drawing his gun reflects an appreciation of the behavior he was about to engage in and its purpose: its purpose was to shoot the President of the United States.

His reflection about his decision to draw the gun: I have referred before to his saying that he thought to himself "Should I?" reflecting on a moral decision he was to make.

And his decision to draw the gun at the very moment he did because of the circumstances which at that time favored a successful assassination: He viewed the situation as having poor security. He saw that the range was close and within the distance with which he was accurate, and at the precise moment that he chose to draw his revolver there was a diversion of attention from him. The Secret Service and the others in the presidential entourage looked the other way just as he was pulling the gun.

Finally, his decision to proceed to fire, thinking that others had seen him, as I have mentioned before, indicates his awareness that others seeing him was significant because others recognized that what he was doing and about to do were wrong.

These are examples of the evidence that he appreciated the wrongfulness on March 30.

Cross Examination by Mr. Fuller

Q. Is it not fair to say that the qualities of emotional coldness, aloofness, cruelness—cruelty, indifference to the feelings of others are features which would go into the whole constellation of features that would bear on the question of one's ability to appreciate the wrongfulness of his conduct?

MR. ADELMAN: Object. May we approach the Bench, Your Honor?

THE COURT: Come to the Bench. . . .

[At the Bench:]

MR. ADELMAN: If the Court please, the basis for this objection is that this question appears to be intending to elicit data relative to emotional appreciation of conduct which has been ruled out. Now that is my understanding of the question. Maybe Mr. Fuller has another idea, but I read it—I listened to the question as seeking to do that. That is my objection.

MR. FULLER: I think it is an appropriate question. The witness has testified that he was able to appreciate the wrongfulness of his conduct. I think it is appropriate to go into the kind of factors that go into that.

MR. ADELMAN: It is not if it goes to emotional factors.

THE COURT: Let's see what he has to say. Very well.

Overruled. . . .

[Dr. Dietz resumed the witness stand.]

MR. FULLER: Your Honor, could I ask that the last question be read by the reporter?

THE COURT: Very well.

[The reporter read the pending question.]

THE WITNESS: My answer to that is no, these are not features that relate to the ability of a defendant to appreciate wrongfulness of his conduct. Indeed, these are features that—the ones you mentioned—that are characteristic of sexual sadists who, while they know it is wrong to mutilate their victims, to remove their viscera, to eat parts of the body, may do so anyway. They do that for other reasons. They enjoy that, and they do it coldly and cruelly.

This issue of emotional coldness is not one that can be translated into a legal concern with appreciation for wrongfulness.

(iv) Hinckley's Capacity to Conform. On the issue of Hinckley's capacity to conform his conduct to the requirements of law, the following testimony was offered.

Dr. William T. Carpenter, Jr., Defense Witness

Direct Examination by Mr. Fuller

Q. [B]ased upon your diagnosis of Mr. Hinckley's mental existence—of the mental disease of Mr. Hinckley on March 30, 1981, do you have an opinion whether at the time of the shooting, which occurred on that date, Mr. Hinckley, as a result of mental disease lacked substantial capacity to [conform] his conduct to the requirements of the law?

A.   Yes, I have an opinion about that.

Q.   Would you please tell us what that opinion is?

A.   Yes. The fact that he had, in my opinion, that he had the illness that I have described to you does not indicate whether at any particular moment he would have had a substantial incapacity to conform his conduct to the requirements of the law. I reach, in my own opinion, I reach the conclusion that he did have a substantial incapacity at that time. The basis for that view deals, of course, with the whole background of psychotic development in his illness that I have described.

And then, more particularly for the point of time in question, was the driven quality to his experiences, the frantic activity that he had become involved in, his determination to end his own life, to terminate this existence that he was experiencing made, foremost in his own mind, actions that would terminate his own life. He experienced the lack of the anchoring, the two anchors that I described,[h] potentially holding him somewhat in contact with reality so that by the time March 30th had arrived he was so dominated, in my opinion, by the inner state that he had developed over a period of time that his actions and the requirement for actions were so extensively determined by this inner state that he was, in my opinion, not able to [conform] his conduct to the outside requirements, to the legal requirements or social requirements of conduct, so that things at that point were completely out of balance for him and it was the driven quality of his inner state that was foremost in determining [his] actions.

And for that reason I reach the opinion that he did have a substantial incapacity in his ability to conform his conduct to the requirements of the law.

Cross Examination by Mr. Adelman

Q.   [Mr. Hinckley was] in a crowd with President Carter at the Dayton Convention Center on the 2nd of October, right?

A.   Yes.

Q.   And you indicate that he was there for the purpose of stalking and shooting President Carter, right?

A.   Yes. The stalking—and that was on his mind, the shooting was on his mind. Whether those were purposes that were involved in this trip

. . .

---

[h] Dr. Carpenter had testified earlier that when Hinckley went to live alone in a motel after meeting his father at the airport on March 7, he had lost his two last "anchors" to reality: "his effort to get psychiatric help [had failed]" and he had "now lost the support of his parents and the relationship with them."

Q. All right. Now you have testified that he got so close according to him that he could shake the President's hand, right?

A. Yes.

Q. And he didn't shoot him, did he?

A. No, he was not armed at the time. He had difficulty—this was a plan that he had just gotten on. He had, as he explained it—did not feel that he was able to take action on it. He partly wanted to get close to President Carter in an effort to see in some sense whether he could psych himself up to where he was able to take action. I don't believe he was armed at the time he was actually that close to Carter.

Q. Did he think he was Travis Bickle on October 2nd in Dayton?

A. He had important aspects of Travis Bickle as part of his makeup through this identification process.

Q. Not my question, not my question.

A. He did not think, literally believe that he was Travis Bickle. What he was doing was finding himself with many attributes of Travis Bickle and content ...

THE COURT: Doctor, on this date in question did he consider—did he think that he was Travis Bickle?

THE WITNESS: No. He experienced himself living out things from the Travis Bickle scenario. He did not literally believe himself to be Travis Bickle.

. . .

Q. On October 2nd, was he under the compulsion which you described that he had on the 30th day of March 1981?

A. Oh, the compulsion at that point was not as intense. There were similarities in the process, but the compulsion to destroy himself and the compulsion to reach this magical union with Jodie Foster was not as intense at that point in October.

Q. But it was there, right?

A. It was there.

Q. He was under some form or degree of this compulsion, right?

A. Yes.

Q. But you said he had to psych himself up, right?

A. Yes. Those are very compatible because I am trying to describe different degrees of intensity.

Q. If he is under a compulsion of some degree, why does he have to psych himself up to do what you say?

A. Because he is not as intensely caught up with it, not as en-thralled and did not feel that he was able to take action. He felt he needed to do things that could prompt him into taking action and this comes [at] a time when he is extremely critical and damning of himself to be unable to take the actions [which] he meant to take when he was there trying to meet Jodie Foster.

So that the process is there. He feels a need for greater intensity of it to enable him to be able to take action. He is not able to take action and the psyching up has to do with degrees in the process, not the presence or absence of the process.

. . . .

Q. All right. Now on October 9, 1980, down there in Nashville, did Mr. Hinckley have process schizophrenia?

A. Yes.

Q. And was he suffering from process schizophrenia when he was before the Police Court in Nashville, Tennessee on that day on the charges of possessing weapons?

A. Yes.

Q. And was he compelled in the fashion that you have mentioned he was on the 2nd of October on the 9th of October?

A. His mental state on those two occasions would have been roughly comparable.

Q. Did he have to psych himself up on the 9th of October to get near President Carter on that day?

A. Psych himself up to get near him, or—get near him, that I said before he tried to get close to President Carter in order to psych himself up, not that he had to psych himself up, to get close to President Carter. He was there. There is an important distinction between the two, because he was—his state of mind was already such that he found himself stalking President Carter and he was stalking him in Dayton and he was stalking him in Nashville. He attempted in Dayton to get close to President Carter to see if he could psych himself up to provoke himself into action so that that is what I am saying that he—his mental state already mobilizes him to get in the area of President Carter.

He tried to get close to him to further psych himself trying to provoke action.

Q. But he wasn't compelled enough that he had to go and shoot the President on that day, right?

A. He didn't.

Q. But the point is he wasn't compelled by this so-called inner world to go shoot the President then, right?

A. Well, the inner world was compelling on him and he did many things there. He did not actually attempt to shoot the President. He didn't find himself then—there will be many occasions where he wished to take action, planned to take action and found himself unable to take action, suicidal action and assassination action. And these would be both Dayton and Nashville, would be examples of this where he is compelled toward that kind of behavior, is not able to culminate the act and does not take action on it.

Q. Because he could conform his behavior to the requirements of the law, couldn't he? He knew it was wrong to shoot presidents and he decided not to do it?

A. No, no. I don't think he was fully conforming his behavior to the requirements of the law. He was carrying illegal weapons. He was stalking and planning an assassination of President Carter. He was not conforming. He did not carry out the act at that time, not because he reasoned to himself it is wrong and I shouldn't do it and was in full control. He carried—he failed to carry it out because he was unable to get himself to do it.

Q. Even though he was compelled by all of these inner world forces, right, that is your testimony?

A. That is right.

. . .

Q. Now you have testified that Mr. Hinckley came here to Washington in late November and stayed here to December 8th, correct?

A. Yes.

Q. And you indicated that he observed, if you will, maybe even stalked the President-elect Reagan and other public officials, right?

A. Yes.

Q. Was he driven by this same compulsion that drove him to Nashville and drove him to Dayton and drove him on March 30th when he was here in December 1980?

A. Well, he was generally driven by the same inner world. It had switched some in content. He lost his interest in President Carter after the election, became more interested in President-elect Reagan, was in general in that same frame of mind. There were—it is the content and some of the themes that are varying over time.

Q. Well, he was here to shoot then-President Reagan if he could, correct?

A. Yes.

He didn't know whether he would shoot him or not. He was here to stalk him. He was here with shooting on his mind. Sometimes he would carry his arms. Sometimes he would not carry his arms. He didn't know what he would do or get done, but on his mind during the time was the stalking and the conversation of the possibility. I don't think during that time that he ever actually was on the verge . . .

Q. My question was, was there ever a time when he was there with his gun when President Reagan was nearby where he could have shot him?

A. Yes.

Q. Yet he didn't, is that correct?

A. Yes.

Q. And he knew the shooting of the President was wrong, right?

A. In the sense we have discussed it, yes.

Q. Right, and he therefore withdrew or controlled himself and didn't give in to the so-called compulsion to shoot the President, did he?

A. That is correct.

. . .

Q. When he got up on the morning of March 30 down at the Park Central Hotel, was he out of control, driven by these internal forces that you have described?

A. These inner forces are driving him to this whole series of behavior that he is now in.

Q. Well, I am asking a particularized question. When he got out of bed that day, when he woke, up, was he out of control, under the compulsion of these inner forces?

A. He was under the compulsion of these inner forces.

Q. In the morning?

A. Throughout this whole period of time.

Q. Okay. Now he woke up roughly at eight o'clock in the morning, didn't he?

A. I think it was about something like that. He had had a fitful night's sleep so he had been awake many times during the night, so it was about eight or so he was getting up.

Q. Nevertheless even though he was under control and being driven by these forces at eight o'clock in the morning, he didn't load his gun and go outside and shoot then?

A. It is not that sort of thing.

Q. He didn't do that?

A. No, he did not do that.

THE COURT: Do you want to explain it, doctor? You say it is "not that sort of thing."

THE WITNESS: Yes. What I am describing is a process, the very fact he is in Washington waking up has to do with this inner drive and these forces, so that it is a process that is taking place over time. At that moment he thinks he is most likely to end in New Haven and some relationship with Jodie Foster and his own death, but there is an inner state. The inner state doesn't come for a second [leading one to ask] why did everything happen then?

It is a process that has been developing over time and it is dominant throughout this. In a process like that, you don't expect that every moment there is going to be a catastrophic act or that the actual barriers of control will come apart. . . . The process is present throughout this period of time, but he did not go out and shoot anybody . . .

Q.   Fine.

A.   . . . at eight o'clock that morning.

Q.   What he did do is go out and have breakfast, right?

A.   That is right.

Q.   Was he under this drive then?

A.   Yes.

Q.   Did he take the gun with him?

A.   I don't think that he took the gun with him when he went out to breakfast.

Q.   Had he loaded the gun by the time he went out for breakfast?

A.   No.

Q.   And he came back and attended to some business in the room, didn't he?

A.   Yes.

Q.   And at one point then—you agree with this—he read in the Washington Star that President Reagan would be at the Hilton Hotel at 1:45, right?

A.   Correct.

Q.   Now was he under this drive that you have described at that very point?

A.   Yes.

Q.   And he read that in the newspaper some two or one and one-half hours before 1:45, didn't he?

A.   Yes.

Q.   And again I ask you as a fact he didn't leave immediately to go with his gun and run up to the Hilton at that point when he read the paper, did he?

A.   No.

Q.   In fact, he loaded his gun thereafter, correct?

A.   Yes, he loaded his gun and then he took preparations for going there.

Q.   And he selected from 43 bullets six bullets to put in the gun didn't he?

A.   Yes.

Q.   Was he under this drive at the time he selected those bullets?

A.   Yes.

Q.   And you know now, don't you, that he selected all of those bullets, six Devastator bullets, correct?

A.   Yes.

Q.   And he specifically loaded Devastator bullets in each of the six chambers of the weapon, right?

A.   Correct.

Q.   Now about what point in time, if you know, did he actually complete the loading of the gun?

A.   I don't know exactly what time that was. That would have been in that period from around 11:30 to 12:30, that after he had read the Star, had taken a shower, and decided he would go over there. He got dressed and loaded the gun and wrote the letter to Jodie Foster during that period of time.

Q.   He planned very carefully, did he not, the loading of the weapon, right?

A.   Yes.

Q.   He made a conscious decision to pick out 6 Devastator bullets as against the other bullets?

A.   That is right.

Q.   And he was able, physically able, to open the weapon and stick the bullets into the chambers?

A.   Yes.

Q.   Then he wrote the letter to Miss Foster, right?

A.   Yes.

. . .

Q.   That letter indicates Mr. Hinckley's then present intent was to go and attempt to kill the President of the United States, does it not?

A.   Yes.

Q.   As a matter of fact, you would agree with me that he had that intent certainly when he read the Washington Star newspaper about an hour or so before, right?

A.   Yes. When he read Washington Star paper and saw the itinerary.

Q.   Right.

A.   He decided to go over with this potential assassination in mind and got settled on that in the few minutes ensuing to go on and see if there were an opportunity to do that and if so, pull it off.

Q.   Your word "settle," that means he thought about it, didn't he?

A.   Yes.

Q.   He turned it over in his mind to consider all the options and possibilities, right?

A.   Oh, he wasn't able to consider a wide range of option possibilities. He did turn it over in his mind and considered some possibilities.

Q.   How many?

A.   He considered the possibility of resting further and then going to New Haven to kill himself and perhaps Jodie Foster, to proceed directly to New Haven that day to [commit] suicide or homicide/suicide, to go to the Hilton to see whether or not he was able to get close to President Reagan and if so, if he would be able to fire at President Reagan and bring this all to an end at that point.

Q.   You are telling us that he had several options spread out in front of him?

A.   Yes, he was able to play out several different options that he could have taken, all of which involved the same conclusion components, which were the termination of his own existence and achieving some magical unification [with] Jodie Foster.

Q.   And you are telling us he selected one of those options from among several, right? He didn't decide that the next thing he would do would be to go to the Hilton to see whether or not that proved to be an option he could act on and if it proved that, to see whether or not he was able to?

A.   He didn't know at the time that he decided to proceed to the Hilton, whether or not he would actually be able to do that, if he got there, would anything happen and just go to New Haven.

At that point he had added this option and then undertook planning to pursue it.

.   .   .

Q.   Now during the time that he was writing a letter, loading the gun and preparing himself at the hotel, was he under the same compulsion that you have described he was when he actually pulled the trigger?

A.   Well, some other things I described that happened at the time that I think played a role in his being able to fully pull the trigger, but the underlying compulsion and drive was present.

Q.   Now was he under the same compulsion when he took the taxicab from the Hotel Park Central up to the Hilton?

A.   Yes.

Q.   Are you aware that he arrived at the Hilton about 1:45 p.m., correct?

A.   Yes, about that or maybe a few minutes before that, 1:30 or 1:45.

Q.   You are aware that he positioned himself close to where the President's limousine would eventually appear, right?

A.   Yes.

Q.   When the President prepared to make an entry into the hotel, was Mr. Hinckley with the gun in his pocket under the same compulsion that he was when he fired the shots?

A.   Well, things—again basically the same compulsion was there. When President Reagan came out of the car, there was a change to some extent in the intensity of it when he had—had that highly personalized experience of feeling that the President was waving and smiling at him.

There was an additional factor that may have played a role in why he was able to take action on this occasion, so things were changing some. Also being in that setting, realized how close he was, how easy it might be to do it. All of these things tend to stir up emotions and to give a different emotional tone.

The basic drive, the basic scenario that he is playing out again is consistent throughout this period of time.

Q.   Let me ask you to focus on the moment when President Reagan leaves the limousine and walks into the hotel. Okay?

A.   Yes.

Q.   Mr. Hinckley was there with the gun, right?

A.   Yes.

Q.   And he could have shot him if he wanted to, right?

A.   Yes.

Q.   But he elected not to shoot him because he didn't have a good shot right?

A.   No, he did not act on that impulse at that moment.

Q.   Well, if the impulse was overwhelming, why didn't he shoot him when he first saw him at 1:45 when he walked into the hotel?

A.   It was the same sort of thing why he didn't shoot himself at the Dakota, why he didn't shoot Reagan early in December and why he didn't shoot Carter. This whole balance of drive and impulse and the thing that makes one hesitate—I think the ability to hesitate has become sharply eroded and I think that personalized experience as Mr. Reagan comes out of the limousine is a further erosion in that, but he did not pull the gun out and fire at that time.

Q.   If the ability to hesitate was eroded when the President got out and waved, why didn't Mr. Hinckley with his ability to hesitate eroded shoot him then?

A.   Because it is not one way or the other and this is the balancing of many factors and there is no way to give you a precise, emphatic answer to why he didn't shoot then, and shot when he came out.

I can describe the alterations that are taking place in his mental state as best I can discern them during that time.

Q.   You mentioned a balancing of factors that means that Mr. Hinckley was considering several options at that particular point?

A.   No, no, no, the balancing, this is part of the entire kind of mind at work. It is not a few things that are isolated out from the rest of one's experience around which they are now weighing out their options the way one might weigh if they are trying to buy a used car and decide if the price is right or not.

It is not a highly reasonable rational, logical "Will I weigh this option against that option?" This is an experience that is taking place. It is happening and it has many, many components, many of which would not be in the conscious mind, his awareness and he is not playing a rational, logical balancing this out.

It is a process that is taking place with many, many components and cannot be isolated to a couple of intellectual decisions about "Do I shoot now" or "Do I hang around a few minutes and shoot later?"

Q.   Look at it this way objectively. He has as an objective matter, the opportunity to shoot the President when he got out of the car, or not to shoot him, correct? He had that option?

A.   Yes.

Q.   And he exercised and made the decision not to shoot him at that point, right?

A.   He did not shoot him at that point.

Q.   And he didn't shoot him because he made, for whatever reason, some decision not to shoot him, right?

A.   Well, maybe I should ask you to define decision. I mean, it is not that he is standing there making decisions. It is like if someone suicides how could you explain why he didn't suicide five minutes ago. He could have done it five minutes ago as well as now. It is not a clear decision-making process that one can isolate then give highly satisfying answers to why did it happen five minutes later instead of then.

He is not there going through decisionmaking processes. He is there living out an experience and he didn't fire at that time. He did fire a few minutes later.

Q.   Doctor, it is fair to say that you, Dr. Carpenter, can't explain why Mr. Hinckley didn't shoot at that point? Is that what your testimony is?

A.   No. I think I could try to give a good deal of information that could help to develop an understanding of why he was there, why the shooting would have taken place and why he was vulnerable to acting on that impulse at that time. I do not have a satisfactory explanation for why did it happen precisely when it did instead of five seconds later [or] instead of 15 minutes before. [It is not possible to give a] precise explanation for why at that moment, not five minutes before, not ten seconds later—[but] I do think that I can give a good deal of information that is relevant to a consideration of why the shooting took place.

Q.   But for that question you have no definitive answer, right?

A.   For why it took place at precisely the moment it did rather than a few seconds earlier or later or rather than ten minutes before? I think it could have taken place before and it didn't. I think he could have found himself unable to act and gone on to New Haven and what, in fact, happened is that he shot as Reagan was leaving the building.

Q.   But that is reasoning from the act back to his mind; isn't that right?

A.   Well—

Q.   Isn't that what you just did?

A.   No. No. There is a lot of reasoning that goes into this. It is not just reasoning from the act.

Q.   All right. Now, during the period when the President—well, do you know how long the President was in the hotel?

A.   I think about 15 or 20 minutes.

Q.   And you know Mr. Hinckley spent part of the time in the lobby of the hotel, correct?

A.   Yes.

Q.   And he made no attempt to break into where the President was speaking to shoot him there, did he?

A.   No.

Q.   Was he under the same compulsion that he was when he fired the shots while he was waiting for the President?

A.   Yes.

Q.   Was he delusional?

A.   Yes.

Q.   Was he process schizophrenic?

A.   Yes.

Q.   You are aware that Mr. Hinckley, while the President was in the speech, then came back and positioned himself at a point close to the President's repositioned limousine, correct?

A.   Yes.

Q.   And as you studied the case, to the extent that you have, you know that Mr. Hinckley put himself where we would get the best shot of Mr. Reagan when he came out?

A.   He put himself at a point where he thought he would be close and where he was in a position to get a shot at Mr. Reagan.

Q.   So he again planned, even up to this point—excuse me, sir— planned even at this point to get himself in the position to do the shooting?

A.   In fact, I think he went back to the same position he had been in before and this was a spot where he could do the shooting he thought.

Q.   You were aware, as he was waiting, as Mr. Hinckley was waiting outside the Hilton he thought, "Should I do this or not," aren't you?

A.   Yes.

Q.   In fact, just so the jury is clear, Dr. Johnson down at Butner, when she interviewed Mr. Hinckley in page 4 of her report, indicated— and I am reading from page 4, Your Honor—"Standing outside the Hilton, the patient remembers thinking 'should I do this or not.'"

.   .   .

Q.   That passage indicates that Mr. Hinckley was thinking whether to do the crime or not, right?

A.   It indicates that.

Q.   Put it either way, he was considering options; is that right?

A.   You have to recognize that this, what is taking place now, is descriptions of something that would have taken place over a few moments in time in someone who had many other things going on in his mind, and he is placing now and describing it as well as he can. He is not—I do not think that that indicates—I think it indicates the dilemma that he is experiencing, "should I do it or not, can I do it or not. What will happen."

Q.   All right.

A.   Again, it is not this kind of considered decisionmaking process that he is weighing his options and figuring out what to do. It is not ordinarily in his mind.

Q.   Now, what I just read to you is not any interpretation, but a quote from Mr. Hinckley, "Should I do this or not."

A.   Yes.

Q.   Six words in ordinary English, right?

A.   Yes.

Q.   And what you just said is your interpretation of that, correct?

A.   No. What I said was that you see Mr. Hinckley is reporting from an extremely complex point in time in his own experience.

Q.   Is that your answer?

A.   No. That is not all of the answer. That he is indicating what he says in those six words does not imply that he can, he is there carefully weighing and balancing different options and thinking it through in some highly rational and reasonable way. It does imply that the thoughts "Should I do this or not" were part of what he had to deal with on his mind at that time.

Q.   And then he made the decision to do it, didn't he?

A.   Well, decision . . .

Q.   Yes or no, sir. Then he decided?

A.   You will have to define decision for me.

Q.   I'll ask the question, if I may.

THE COURT: No. Now wait just a second. Do you understand the question?

THE WITNESS: Well, I understand the question, but I can't quite answer. I think I can do it briefly, but not yes or no. You see, Mister . . .

THE COURT: What is it you do not understand about the question?

THE WITNESS: Well, the question that then he made a decision to fire implies that it is an ordinary, intellectual process that he made a decision and then did it the way one might make a decision to purchase something then indicate they want to make a purchase.

THE COURT: Answer the question as you perceive it.

THE WITNESS: Okay. No. In those terms, I do not think that he made the decision and did it. I believe that he found himself in the impulse of that moment firing at President Reagan.

. . .

Q.   Doctor, would you be kind enough to pull out your report, the November 13 report?

A.   Surely.

Q.   ... Now this report, this portion of the report contains your description of Mr. Hinckley's thought processes and behavior at the time of the shooting; does it not?

A.   Yes.

Q.   I want to establish one point here.

You write as follows describing Mr. Hinckley and what he did and what he thought after the President went in the hotel: "He went to the hotel lobby for a few minutes and then came outside for fresh air"—and here is where I want to pause—"and debated what to do"; right?

A.   Yes.

Q.   You use the word "debated" in your report, right?

A.   Yes.

Q.   Now you have indicated that Mr. Hinckley was on March 30, 1981, at the Hilton Hotel, driven. More particularly, as you have testified [that there was a] "driven quality to his experiences, the frantic activity that he had become involved in, his determination to end his own life, to terminate this existence that he was experiencing made, foremost in his own mind, actions that would terminate his own life."

Right?

A.   Yes.

Q.   Now you maintained in your testimony here in this court, Mr. Hinckley shot at the President of the United States and the other victims in part [as a way] to end his own life, a suicide act; correct?

A.   Yes.

Q.   If Mr. Hinckley was driven to commit suicide, could he not have shot himself in the room with a gun at the Park Central Hotel? Couldn't he have done that?

A.   He couldn't. He had tried to shoot himself. You see there is more than one thing operative and he had also failed in suicide attempts before, the Dakota [incident of November 1980] being a recent one. He was driven to accomplish both the magical union [with] Jodie Foster and the termination of his existence, and had found himself unable to do that simply by killing himself and, of course, that was one of the plans that he was debating, whether he could shoot himself if he tried to do it in front of Jodie Foster, if he went on to New Haven.

Q.   He was driven to commit suicide. Couldn't he have gone up to the Hilton Hotel and simply pulled the gun out and shot in the air and had the Secret Service take care of him? He could have done that, couldn't he?

A. Well, I mean in a hypothetical sense he could have done thousands of different ways to [commit] suicide in a hypothetical sense. In terms of his own inner state and how he was conducting his life at that point that was not an option that he experienced.

Q. He wanted to commit suicide up at the Hilton Hotel?

A. I have explained that he wanted more . . .

Q. I have another question.

A. . . . than commit suicide.

Q. If he wanted to commit suicide at the Hilton Hotel, couldn't he have gone up there with the toy gun that was in his room and pulled it out and let the Secret Service blow him away? He could have done that, couldn't he?

A. You see, I am not presenting him as having only one single motivation in mind. I have said that foremost in his mind is to accomplish the termination of this experience, his existence. He is driven toward accomplishing the unification with Jodie Foster, the assassination of President Reagan in his mind, the way he put this together is a way to accomplish something with her, simply suicide at the Hilton and these other things which he did not consider.

So far as I know, he did not consider doing it with the plastic gun but the point I am trying to make is that he is trying to accomplish several things that are dictates of this inner world, not simply suicide.

He is also trying to prompt himself into action that will do this.

Q. On March 30, he was trying to prompt himself.

A. Yes.

Q. Trying to psych himself up?

A. Trying to get himself in sort of the whole trip he is, he is going after circumstances that he thinks may enable him to take action so he is looking for circumstances. He feels the need for circumstances that can enable him to take action so often having failed, having been [un]able to take action before, so he is seeking out circumstances that can prompt him into action.

Q. I ask you a specific question: On March 30, 1981, did Mr. Hinckley psych himself up to do the act that he eventually did?

A. In the way I have used "psyched up" and understood it from the failure before, I would say that Mr. Hinckley was already in a psyched up state of mind. And in proceeding to Washington and planning to go to New Haven, that he already felt psyched up, that he still feels the need for circumstances that [can] accomplish his aims and that prompts him into action.

Q. How long had he been psyched up?

A.   Well, I think psyched up for this final, probably he had made, he had felt desperate when he left Denver. You can imagine one final constructive effort to be able to bring some closure to this experience in life that would not be destructive and that was the trip to California in the effort to sell his music and the next morning was leaving.

I think having given up on [what] was the last imaginable ... constructive outcome, that he did not expect to live, that he was psyched up from that point on and did not expect to live much longer and saw himself bringing this to a close in the way he had planned it out.

Q.   Finally, when he fired the shots, was he under this driven compulsion to do the act?

A.   Yes.

Q.   You are aware that Mr. Hinckley took a command action position and fired the gun in this fashion I am crouching.

A.   Yes.

Q.   And you are aware that he was able to hit four people with six shots; right?

A.   Yes.

Q.   He didn't fire wildly about the street in any fashion, did he?

A.   No, he didn't wildly. I don't think that he was trying to hit each of the four people he hit, but he was not firing wildly. He was discharging the pistol as rapidly as he could and did hit four people.

Q.   Mr. Hinckley told you, did he not, that he shot at the car?

A.   I don't think that he is certain what he shot at at the time. He told me that he thought he might have diverted his aim at the last moment and aimed at the limousine instead.

Q.   Did you believe him when he told you that?

A.   I think that may have happened that way, but I am not convinced and I wouldn't be able to present an opinion, a convincing opinion, one way or the other on that.

Dr. Park Elliott Dietz, Government Witness

Direct Examination by Mr. Adelman

Q.   [L]et me ask you formally, if you determined whether at the time of the criminal conduct on March 30, 1981, the defendant Hinckley, as a result of mental disease or defect, lacked substantial capacity to conform his conduct to the requirements of the law?

A.   I did make such a determination.

Q.   What determination did you make?

A.   That on March 30, 1981, as a result of mental disease or defect, Mr. Hinckley did not lack substantial capacity to conform his conduct to the requirements of the law.

. . .

Q.   . . . Can you give us the evidence, some of the evidence which underlies your answer?

A.   Yes, I can. . . . Among the reasons, the pieces of evidence, for my opinion that Mr. Hinckley was able to conform his conduct on March 30, 1981, are, again, the background. I have reviewed for you some of the evidence that he was capable of deliberation, of planning, that he had backed out in the past despite his efforts to "psych himself up."

This background indicates that in the past he had conformed his behavior, that he had had the ability to do so and had, in fact, done so. He hadn't drawn a gun in Dayton, perhaps because he didn't carry one with him. He hadn't drawn a gun in Nashville, and at Blair House in Washington he hadn't shot. He says he thought to himself on those occasions that he could do it another time. His ability to control his conduct on those dates to conform to the requirements of the law is part of the background for how it is that we know that he had that ability on March 30th.

At no point has Mr. Hinckley stated to me that he had a compulsion or a drive to assassinate or to commit other crimes.

Now, specific examples of evidence:

First of all, his decisionmaking ability itself was [intact] on March 30th. He was able to make other decisions on that date. He decided where to go for breakfast, what to eat. He decided to buy a newspaper, to shower. He made personal decisions of that sort. He was not a man incapable on that day of making decisions about his life, about which of these relatively minor things to do.

He deliberated and made a decision to survey the scene at the Hilton Hotel. There was no voice commanding him to do that. There was no drive within him pushing him to do that. He decided, as he tells us, to go to the Hilton to check out the scene to see how close he could get.

We know from the facts that he chose his bullets, that he loaded his revolver. He has never said that a voice commanded him to choose the shiniest bullets or that he had, for some other reason, to choose these. He indicated that he chose them randomly. And we know that is not so. He chose the exploding [Devastator] bullets. This reflects decisionmaking and choice.[i] He is controlling his conduct, is taking the time to write the "Jodie letter" to explain that one of his goals for the assassination

---

[i] The evidence showed that Hinckley loaded his gun with six exploding Devastator bullets and left 35 round-nosed bullets and two hollow-point bullets behind in his hotel room. [Footnote by eds.]

attempt, and to explain that he had a deliberate reason for carrying it out. A man driven by passion, by uncontrollable forces, is not often inclined to take the time to write a letter to explain what this is about. He did. And he claims he spent 20 to 35 minutes writing that letter.

He concealed the weapon not only from Mrs. Kondeah [the maid at the hotel], but from people in the hotel lobby, from taxi drivers, from people at the scene at the Hilton, until the moment he chose to draw his weapon. That ability to conceal his weapon is further evidence of his conforming his conduct, that is, he recognized that [w]aving a gun would be behavior likely to attract attention, and did not wave the gun. He concealed it.

His ability to wait, when he did not have a clear shot of the President on the President's way into the Hilton is further evidence of his ability to conform his behavior. A man driven, a man out of control, would not have the capacity to wait at that moment for the best shot.

His lack of desperation that day, and his recognition that he had other options: I haven't told you all the evidence of that yet, but he has indicated on a number of occasions what some of his options were. He considered going to New Haven, Connecticut. He considered going back to his hotel and going to sleep. These are options. He chose which option to carry out.

His ability to wait in the crowd until the entourage exited the Hilton: now, he waited inside, he says, and then exited taking up the spot he had occupied previously. He went back to the same place outside the Hilton Hotel and indicates that he didn't have very long to wait there. But he did go back out, he had waited 'til that point, and he went outside, and he waited again until the President came out.

He says that he gave consideration to not firing after he had pulled the gun, and of course he said that he deliberated whether to pull the gun.

These choices, his description of deliberation, of decisionmaking, indicate that he was conforming his conduct to his own wishes, that he had the ability to control, to think, to decide, and that he did so. He controlled his conduct. He decided what to do, and he carried out his goals.

His having waited for the very moment to pull his gun and seizing that moment to fire the six shots, again indicates not a man who is willed, but a man who chooses the precise moment when his opportunity for assassination is best.

He took aim at the President, not, as he says, not aiming. He is seen in the videotapes in a combat crouch with a two-handed hold on the gun, the gun pointed toward the President, tracking the President's movements. These are organized acts. These are not disorganized random motions. These are specifically designed, organized acts.

Those are examples of the evidence supporting Mr. Hinckley having had the capacity to conform his conduct on March 30.

Cross Examination By Mr. Fuller

Q.   Now, it is accurate, is it not, Doctor, that a psychotic condition is not indispensable to a finding that an accused's ability to [conform] his conduct to the requirements of the law is impaired?

A.   It is correct that a person need not be found psychotic for a Court to find that . . . the individual has substantially impaired capacity to conform.

. . .

Q.   Is it not accurate that you concluded, you and your colleagues, referring to the behavior of Mr. Hinckley which eventuated in the shootings of March 30, 1981, "it is quite clear that these are not the reasonable acts of a completely rational individual?"

A.   We did conclude that. That is correct.

Q.   And that, going on, your "opinion about the legal question of criminal responsibility—and it is only an opinion, for the final determination is for the jury—does not hinge on psychiatric diagnoses or speculations?"

A.   That is absolutely correct, that our opinion is just our opinion— it is for the jury to determine—and that our opinion isn't based on psychiatric diagnoses or speculation.

Q.   And that you indicated Mr. Hinckley's history is clearly indicative of a person who did not function in a usual reasonable manner?

A.   That's right. That is why we have diagnosed him as having these disorders.

Q.   And you go on to say, "However, there is no evidence that he was so impaired that he could not appreciate the wrongfulness of his conduct or conform his conduct to the requirements of the law," is that correct?

A.   Yes, it is.

Q.   And . . . you describe options available to Mr. Hinckley on March 30, 1981, is that correct?

A.   Yes.

Q.   And again I am quoting: "At that time, as at previous times, there were options available to Mr. Hinckley that did not involve the shooting of the President," is that correct?

A.   Yes, it is.

Q.   "Some of the alternatives that he considered were to commit suicide alone . . ." Is that correct?

A.   Yes.

Q.   "... to go to New Haven and murder himself in front of Miss Foster?"

A.   Yes.

Q.   " ... or to return to his hotel room and reconsider his plans"?

A.   Those are the ones we listed. My colleagues convinced me to take out the one where he told us he considered coming in out of the rain.

THE COURT: Coming in out of the rain?

THE WITNESS: Yes sir. At one point he said he "just wasn't that desperate." It was raining outside, and he considered going in out of the rain instead of shooting the President.

BY MR. FULLER:

Q.   And you indicated that "Mr. Hinckley stated that if the President had not come out of his speech so quickly, he would not have ..."

MR. ADELMAN: Objection. Counsel has skipped a sentence. Would he be kind enough to read that sentence, please?

THE COURT: You asked him what he said, Mr. Fuller.

BY MR. FULLER:

Q.   "He elected consciously and volitionally not to choose any of these alternatives despite the absence of any compelling drive to choose the course of action that he chose." Is that correct?

A.   Yes, it is.

Q.   "In fact, Mr. Hinckley stated if the President had not come out from the speech so quickly, he would not have stood around waiting, but instead would have returned to his hotel and reconsidered his plan to go to New Haven." Is that correct?

A.   Yes, it is.

MR. FULLER: I have no further questions.

3. Closing Argument. At the end of the testimony, the lawyers for both sides, as is customary, were permitted to make closing arguments to the jury. Excerpts from these arguments follow.

Closing Argument by Mr. Adelman for the Government

[The defendant] stalked two Presidents. Jimmy Carter in October of 1980. [W]e now learn he allegedly stalked President Reagan at the Blair House downtown in Washington in December. He target practiced....

What is he target practicing for? To kill himself? You don't need to target practice to kill yourself. What is he target practicing with different caliber ammunition for? To pick the best weapon, the deadliest weapon. He found it. A .22 loaded with Devastator bullets.

It was also planned and premeditated in that he practiced, he thought about it. Dr. Dietz told you of his interest in assassination.... His interest in fame. His interest in famous crimes.... Mr. Hinckley admitted that he had thoughts of assassinating President Reagan as early as December of 1980.

I'm saying this to you to show you that this wasn't a wild, thoughtless, out of control act by a man who couldn't control his behavior. In fact, at 1:45 when Mr. Reagan arrived, Mr. Hinckley is standing there. There he is in (indicating exhibit). And he doesn't shoot then. He waited for the best shot.... At 1:45 it was not the best opportunity because the evidence shows us, does it not, that Mr. Reagan's limousine was pulled close to the Hilton. Mr. Hinckley didn't have a good shot.

[T]he evidence shows, Mr. Hinckley admitted, and it is in writing in the record—[that] during the period of time when the President was in the hotel he said, "Should I do it? Should I not?" He is thinking, deliberating, planning, if you will. What is the "it"? Buy a soda? Go to the bathroom? No. Shoot the President.

He decided to do it. And when the time came to shoot him, he said.... "I'll never have a better opportunity." ... When you look at the videotape you see a Secret Service agent walks right up to Mr. Hinckley and turns to the left and it is at that point after the agent turns his back away that Mr. Hinckley pulls out the gun and fires.

Appreciate wrongfulness of his conduct and conform his behavior to the requirements of the law? You better believe it. This man was out of control or in a frenzy? Why wouldn't he pull the gun and start firing right away? Would he be able to shoot as accurately as he did? Would he be able to hit four people with [six] shots with a .22? That is what I mean by common sense. That is what I mean by common sense.

Finally, it is important to remember the choice of weapon here indicates that he had to be near the victim. Twenty feet was the range. You can see by the pictures, the President was no more than ten or 15 feet away.

Now, everything I'm going to say hereafter this morning and this afternoon has a foundation on these facts of the crime.

I want you to keep that in mind because this indictment doesn't talk about anything else than March 30, 1981, or anything else than is depicted in this evidence. He is not charged here with being sad at Christmas. He is not charged here with going to the Dakota Apartment building in New York in February. He is not even charged here with stalking President Carter in Nashville or President Carter out in Dayton. He is charged with 13 crimes that happened at 2:20 p.m. on the 30th of March.

That's the issue in this case and let us see as the day progresses how much the defense tells you about that.

The defense is allegedly that of criminal responsibility. I think you have heard every witness questioned about the two parts [of the test]. It is important that you know that because "part one" has to do with whether the man had a mental disease or defect. Mental disorder as the doctors call it.

[T]he defense presentation ... is concerned [only] about part one. [Part two concerns] whether [Hinckley's] ability to appreciate wrongfulness or conform his behavior to the requirement of the law was substantially impaired. The defense never bothered to deal with that question. Why? Because they can't. Because they can't. All these doctors' CAT scans, delusion, fantasies and everything else. Miles away from that question.

[T]he evidence shows, and the Government doesn't contend otherwise that on March 30, 1981, Mr. Hinckley had mental disorders....

Well, now, does that mean he is not responsible? No way. The question is whether that substantially interfered with his ability to appreciate or conform. All the doctors who testified on that score for the Government ... pointed out to you that the mere existence of a mental disorder doesn't mean that you are not criminally responsible.

These disorders that the Government doctors testified they found in Mr. Hinckley [are] personality disorders. Are they severe mental disorders? They could be. Were they severe in Mr. Hinckley? No, they were not. What are personality disorders? They don't make you out of contact with reality. Not delusional. [They are] things that hundreds of thousands of people have. I think we all had a laugh when Dr. Dietz said that this narcissistic personality even applies to some doctors. We didn't count noses on that one, but I think we could all put it on some of the psychiatrists.

I don't mean to demean psychiatrists or doctors. I'm trying to show you that the diagnosis of Mr. Hinckley doesn't meet the qualifications. But the Government doctors say, and clearly I think the evidence supports that, whatever disorders [he had] were certainly not severe ones.

Let me put it another way. There is a whole spectrum of mental disorders. There is a whole spectrum of physical disorders. If you have the sniffle and a head cold, that is one thing. If you have double pneumonia, you have trouble. I'm not trying to equate the two, but I'm trying to let you know, as the evidence shows, there is a considerable spectrum and ... it is not evident that [Hinckley] had any serious mental disorder on that day.

Now, the defense. Let me talk for a moment about what the defense is offering on this score....

Isn't it interesting right from the opening statement of the defense, when Mr. Fuller stood up, you didn't hear about March 30, 1981. You heard about fantasies, Mr. Hinckley's background, mother, father, parents, family, good people, Texas Tech, writing, all these things. Jodie Foster. You didn't hear anything about March 30, 1981. . . .

· · ·

In [the cross-examination of Dr. Dietz] how much did you hear counsel for defense ask him about March 30, 1981? I don't recall very much. I will leave it up to you. Why is this? Why is this? It is obvious, isn't it? Your common sense tells you why. Because they can't look this fact in the face. They can't look this fact in the face. John Hinckley shooting the President. They can't look that fact in the face. See the question of responsibility, criminal responsibility, and the defense simply doesn't want to deal with it because the evidence, I submit to you, is clear, direct, and overwhelming.

· · ·

John Hinckley led an ordinary American life. The parents loved him. There is no question about that.

A brother and sister, who he respected and admired, even envied. These people didn't offer any evidence that he suffered a serious mental disorder.

Yes, they told you he was a loner. He was sad. . . . Dr. Dietz indicated to you that loneliness is perhaps the most common phenomenon in the United States and depression or sadness probably runs No. 2.

All you have to do is turn on any radio station and listen to it for half an hour. How many songs are you going to hear about these themes? We are not trivializing this, not a bit.

John was especially lonely. He was especially sad. In fact, that special sadness—well, it is now a dollar term, I guess with inflation—dysthymic disorder. That is a Greek word that means "sad mood."

But these problems didn't prevent Mr. Hinckley from functioning from day to day, did it? Mr. Hinckley didn't want to work, but that wasn't because he was psychotic, but because he wanted money from his parents, his sense of entitlement.

Mr. Hinckley wanted to go chase after Jodie Foster. That is not because he was delusional or delirious. It was because he had the time to do it. Nobody made him work. He didn't have to.

You know, look at those charts (indicating). [They show] Mr. Hinckley flying all over the United States. This man is not a drifter or a loner stumbling around some little town in Nebraska running into fence posts. He is flying United Airlines, he is flying American. He took the limousine, if you will, on March 6, 1981, from New York to Newark Airport.

This is probably enough miles there to qualify for the 10,000–Mile Club in some of these airlines.

Did you ever hear any evidence that Mr. Hinckley didn't have the ability to make the airline connections, to travel around and do what he wanted?

This chart proves one thing, that John Hinckley was—even you and I have trouble getting through United and doing things we have to do to get around. This doesn't prove Mr. Hinckley is mentally disordered. It also proves, by the way, he is very interested in Jodie Foster, just like any other fan would be. Just like any other young man with a fantasy.

These aren't mental defects. An obsession is not that either.

.   .   .

Dr. Dietz and his team concluded that Mr. Hinckley has three personality disorders, and this sadness disorder called dysthymic disorder.

Now, I am not going to go through all that again, but they concluded he wasn't delusional, had no psychosis or anything of that character.

Dr. Dietz spent, I believe, two hours telling you why on March 30, 1981, Mr. Hinckley was criminally responsible. Why he could appreciate wrongfulness. Why he could conform his behavior. Why he could understand what he was doing.

Now, Dr. Dietz also explained that these mental disorders are a narcissistic personality, mixed personality disorder, and the other one, a big long name, are very common things, and I told you before that many of these personality disorders are found [in] hundreds and thousands of people. Mr. Hinckley is not unusual.

Do you know what happened in this case, really, from all doctors? Mr. Hinckley I submit to you, is an ordinary person that has been put under a microscope. Microscope of defense doctors and microscope of Government doctors, and what did that show? That he is an ordinary person.

Now, Dr. Dietz also indicated to you that there are certain matters or fantasies which everybody has, daydreams and the like, delusions which are serious thought disorders which reality won't change. Hallucinations [such as] hearing voices, and obsessions and preoccupations and the like. Mr. Hinckley has . . . never had any delusion about Jodie Foster or anybody else. Mr. Hinckley never reported hallucinations to anybody except for Dr. Carpenter who sat down with him and talked to him so long about these voices. . . .

Now, Dr. Dietz said a couple of other important things I would like to bring to your attention. . . . First of all, he studied Mr. Hinckley longitudinally. In other words, from early on, all the way to the end, and he did that by talking to Mr. Hinckley, a lot of interviews, and also checking out with what he said in writing, with his parents and brother and sister, and he said Mr. Hinckley had a strong desire for fame, fame.

Why? Well, you can draw your own conclusions. I suggest to you Mr. Hinckley developed that over the years because he was sort of the fifth wheel. Scott, a successful businessman and his brother. Diane, successful daughter. Marriage, two children now, I believe, and there is John Hinckley, sort of loping beside. His dad, a successful businessman. John Hinckley wanted to be somebody. He wanted to be like John Lennon, but John Hinckley, said Dr. Dietz, wanted to do this easy. He didn't want to work. He wanted to get his inheritance, if you will, and just wanted to go that route.

That is John Hinckley's route.

Dr. Dietz also suggested to you that ... John Hinckley had an interest in famous crimes, and he studied carefully over the years famous crimes. Skyjacking, shootings, things of that sort, assassination, all of those.

Why? Because he was interested in that and ultimately, said Dr. Dietz, [he] selected and chose and discarded and decided upon a crime to commit, and he did commit it on March 30, 1981. This is the deliberation, the pre-thought. Deliberation. Pre-thought. Certainly not insanity. Certainly not schizophrenia.

. . .

Ladies and gentlemen, on the critical day of March 30, which I have talked so much about, we have reached the point where Mr. Hinckley had loaded the weapon. I am discussing all of this in the context of the evidence, testimony, the expert testimony, and how it shows his ability to conform his behavior and to appreciate wrongfulness.

Now, the next important thing that happened, Mr. Hinckley wrote a letter [which is] in evidence, that Jodie letter. He wrote this letter, according to the note on it, at 12:45, about an hour or two hours before the crime, a little less.

This evidence, this letter in his handwriting, among all the other evidence clearly shows to you ... a clear awareness of what he was thinking about doing, and as the evidence shows from the experts and I will talk about it in a minute, a clear understanding that what he was about to do was wrong, a clear indication that he could conform his behavior to the requirements of the law.

In the first paragraph of the letter he is writing to Jodie Foster. He says, "There is a definite possibility I will be killed in my attempt to get Reagan." This is written at 12:45, an hour and a half before. Doesn't that clearly show in his own handwriting, in his own handwriting, his acknowledgement of the wrongfulness of what he is doing? He understands that he will get killed, perhaps, in his attempt to get Reagan. He understands that it is wrong. Simple logic. . . .

Finally, you have heard enough about this letter and you can look at it, if you like, to see in contrast to what the defense doctors would have you believe. This man was perfectly rational, perfectly organized at the time he wrote this letter.

You take a look at it.

As Dr. Dietz pointed out and as you will see, the words are in order. There is nothing—run-on sentences, paragraphs very well, everything is logically written. Is this the letter of a man who is driven, who can't control his behavior, who has an inner rage ... who is suffering from some problem in his inner world? Would a person who has that problem write a letter like this?

[The] letter wasn't mailed. Remember, it is found in the hotel room in an envelope. If this man was driven to do this crime, if he had [been] compelled, if he had no choice, would[n't] he have mailed the letter as his final statement to Jodie Foster? Dr. Johnson pointed out that the fact that he didn't mail the letter fits into the pattern of John Hinckley of not being sure whether he was going to go through with the crime.

He didn't know if the situation up at the hotel would be right. What does that signify? Planning, consideration, reflection, appreciation of wrongfulness, conforming to law. At the time he wrote the letter he wasn't sure he was going to do it.

Still, the opportunity, the option, the ability and the fact of making choices. The letter not being mailed shows—in other words, as the doctor put it, [his] appreciation of the inherent risk of what he was about to do.

You see, if he mailed the letter we might have a different situation. As I said, the letter reveals not only appreciation in one sense, but it also reveals that he might lose his freedom, be locked up, be shot, be killed by the Secret Service or the police or whoever are up there.

And finally, [Hinckley was] committed to the prospect of leaving a letter at the crime scene.

Why is that significant? First of all, it underscores the accuracy of the diagnosis that both Dr. Johnson and Dr. Dietz and their respective teams really came to.

Mr. Hinckley's narcissistic personality, the theme, the fame, the desire for importance. This is John Hinckley going down in a blaze of glory. Blaze of glory. He left a note for Jodie Foster. Doesn't this tie in with what he told [the police after his arrest]: "You go to my hotel room. You go to my hotel room." This isn't John Hinckley in a delusion. This is John Hinckley desiring fame.

Dr. Johnson said, Dr. Dietz said, the conclusions of both of those groups of doctors is that Mr. Hinckley desired to be famous, important and well known.

And unfortunately, as we have four victims you know about, he succeeded. He succeeded and he told Dr. Dietz that.

Let's go on. He left the hotel and took a taxicab again calculating the time, the place and so forth. He didn't know Washington too well, we can assume, but he made it up there. He hid the weapon. There is certainly clear evidence of that. Mrs. Kondeah, she didn't see it. We have no indication he pulled it out on the cab driver. We have no indication he pulled it out when he got up there.

What is the significance of that? It is illegal to carry a weapon here in Washington anyway. Doesn't it show his ability to conform to the law to hide the weapon? Doesn't it show his appreciation of wrongfulness of that act to hid the weapon? You see, if he is walking around up there at the Hilton with a .22 in his hand we might have a different situation.

Then we have John Hinckley on the way, still considering the possibilities of shooting the President, going to New Haven or just going on. [T]his speaks to his appreciation of the wrongfulness. The opportunity to make decisions.

And also on the way to the Hilton and, indeed, before, there is one other important factor, too. John Hinckley was aware, he knew, he told [the psychiatrists] that he knew that his range, if you will, his accuracy was limited to 20 or 30 feet and this ties into what happened at the Hilton. Very significant when John Hinckley showed up. Oh, by the way, here he is [pointing to photograph]. This driven man, see how driven he is here. See the inner world. It is not there....

My point is when he got to the Hilton he stood outside in that line at about 1:45. Mr. Reagan appeared at 1:50. If he was so driven, if he was so compelled he couldn't control behavior, why didn't he shoot him then? You know the answer. He wasn't. He wasn't compelled. He could conform his behavior to law. He could appreciate the wrongfulness.

Indeed, he waited until he got in the best position. We heard testimony that the limousine and Mr. Reagan were not in a good position for him to shoot. He knew that, he calculated that....

Mr. Hinckley, at 1:45 or 1:50, assessed the situation. Now, that word means [that] you think about it. You turn it over in your mind. He assessed it. And he decided; he made the decision not to shoot.

And remember, during the time the President was in the hotel giving the speech did Mr. Hinckley leave? Did he go away? Did he follow him in the hotel? No, he waited outside. And what we know from the testimony of Dr. Dietz [is] that Mr. Hinckley said that at that point he was thinking, should I, should I do what? Should I shoot the President of the United States? Should I go to Yale and see Jodie Foster or should I go somewhere else? Making decisions all along, debating, indicating consciousness of decision.

Those are from Mr. Hinckley's own lips, ladies and gentlemen.....

And you see, you don't hear any of this from the defense doctors. Nobody from the defense side of the house talks to you about these things. This is the bread and butter. This is the meat and potatoes that proves from Mr. Hinckley's own statements appreciation of wrongfulness and conformity to law....

Now, this is a man, we are told by the defense, [who] is driven, compelled and what have you. He checked out the police. He noticed that the police for some reason were across the street. Across the street, if you know that part of town, but yet they weren't right near where the press line was and he noticed the positioning of the Secret Service agents. Why is he doing that? If this man is driven and compelled, would he care? If he has this inner turmoil going on, would he care? If he is psychotic, would he care?

Whatever Mr. Hinckley was thinking, he was clearly thinking about the concern with the police.

Finally, ... Mr. Hinckley knew just before the President came out that if he moved or lunged or did something to go up beyond the press line into where the President was directly, he would be apprehended. Yet another occasion of appreciation, knowledge of wrongfulness and ability to conform his behavior because he didn't do that. He merely waited.

He was deliberate and careful. He was so careful when Mr. Reagan came out of the hotel he waited for the best and only clear shot and the videotape shows you that and I told you this morning exactly what that videotape indicated.

He also told Dr. Johnson that he debated even at the last moment whether to shoot and he made the decision to shoot and he did.

And the bottom line here is, as I have told you earlier, he [told] Dr. Johnson on April 3rd, within a week of the crime, "I'll never have a better opportunity." That is what his mind was saying, that is what he was thinking. That is not the thought of a driven man. That is not the thought of a man who can't control his behavior.

That is a deliberative, determinative thought. And he shot not just once, six times. And he didn't shoot wildly as I have told you. He didn't shoot all over the street into the ground, into the car. For goodness sake, some of these defense doctors believe his statement that he was shooting at the limousine. You can see that he didn't. He shot directly at his target six times and in the course of that he hit four innocent people with the weapon that he carefully practiced and trained with....

And finally, if any more evidence be needed, what does Mr. Hinckley say about this particular issue at this time up at the Hilton? Now, a man who the defense would have you believe is driven and frenzied, out of control, said—and the evidence bears this out in an interview with Dr. Dietz or one of his colleagues—as follows: "If I was going to have to wait within five or ten minutes, I was going to go back to the hotel. I just wasn't that desperate about it." That is Mr. Hinckley talking. No doctor said that, no policeman said that.

"I just wasn't that desperate about it." He repeats, "I just wasn't that desperate to act that afternoon." Is that a driven man? By his own admission, by his own admission he wasn't.

And then he said, "That just wasn't my plan." "Plan," that is his word, "plan." Also he says "It was raining and I wasn't going to stand around in the rain. It was misting."

Now, if you are driven, if you are frenzied, if you are compelled, are you going to be forced away by the rain and the mist? I submit to you, I submit to you that is the end of it. And that is Mr. Hinckley.

Dr. Johnson also told you that after March 30th when she examined Mr. Hinckley during her 120–day period during those 55 interviews, during the other sessions with other doctors at her prison team there, he was never psychotic, never out of touch with reality, had a good memory about what happened on March 30th and she said that Mr. Hinckley, when she examined him from time to time, as she sat there looking at him, you know, face to face, that his mental condition was just the same or even worse than it was on March 30th. And Dr. Johnson said, "He wasn't out of control when I talked to him, he wasn't psychotic. He wasn't unable to conform his behavior to the law."

Now, ladies and gentlemen, I have had the opportunity to summarize evidence that has transpired over the last eight weeks and the opportunity will continue after defense counsel speaks. . . .

When you hear defense counsel, hear him out and listen carefully and see how much of what he says is about, or relates to, March 30, 1981. Because when all is said and done, that is the critical date. At 2:25 p.m. on that date is the critical time.

When all is said and done, the plain, simple, unvarnished facts in this case [are] that at that time and place this man, John Hinckley, shot four people right down on the street at close range.

He shot the President in the chest. He shot Mr. Brady in the head, Mr. Delahanty in the back, Mr. McCarthy in the chest. Those are the facts and the evidence undisputed.

I suggest to you the defense in this case so far hasn't confronted those facts, hasn't dealt with those facts and there are no amount of psychiatrists, psychologists, writings, relatives, anybody else, movies, what have you, Jodie Fosters, in the world to come in and confront the evidence that I have presented to you.

No amount of these things, no amount of these psychiatrists or tests or writings or poems or lyrics or what you have, can deny from this evidence a conclusion that John Hinckley is guilty of each and every one of these crimes and that John Hinckley is responsible, criminally responsible for each and every one of these crimes.

You see, it all comes back to what I said this morning. It all comes back to what John Hinckley said. He said, speaking of himself with gun in hand up there at the Hilton, "I will never have a better opportunity."

Thank you.

Closing Argument by Mr. Fuller for the Defense

May it please the Court, ladies and gentlemen of the jury.

[Y]ou will be charged with the responsibility of determining defendant John Hinckley's responsibility, legal responsibility for the acts of March 30, 1981.

. . .

[The government's] psychiatrists chose to ignore the kind of existence this defendant lived in in the seven years prior to March of 1981.

Don't be misled by Mr. Adelman's suggestion that only March 30, 1981, should be considered. Is there any way in this world that Mr. Hinckley or anybody else would become instantly insane on March 30, 1981? It took years and years of growth of the disease or disorder to lead to the state of mind on March 30, 1981. So do not be misled by Mr. Adelman's challenge that I should focus only on March 30, 1981, because the question is not only what was he like then, but to show what he was like, we must look at how he got there.

I believe the Government psychiatrists played that down. I think they also trivialized the frenetic behavior of the defendant over the months preceding the tragedy of March 30, 1981. You look at the Government's charts. . . . You look at the absolutely absurd travel pattern pursued by this man starting on September 17th and running through March of 1981. On its face, it is irrational, purposeless, aimless.

[According to the government's experts, the defendant focused in March on various options] as alternatives to shooting the President: commit suicide, to go to New Haven and murder Miss Foster and go to New Haven and murder himself in front of Miss Foster or return to his hotel.

I suggest to you, ladies and gentlemen, these are very strange options if they are offered as evidence of the sanity, the lack of mental disease, the lack of psychotic disease. . . .

Ladies and gentlemen of the jury, I submit to you that Mr. Hinckley at the time of these events was living in such a self-contained world with no outside checks, no possibility of there being any realities, that he was unaware of anything except his goal and his goal was to achieve the love and admiration of Jodie Foster.

. . .

I want to call to mind several things Mr. Adelman said in his opening remarks. He characterized the defendant at one point as an ordinary person like any other young man, an all American boy like any other fan. These are characterizations made by Mr. Adelman at different times during the morning.

Ladies and gentlemen, that is patently absurd. This defendant is unique in this sense: He lived a solitary life. He was a prisoner of himself for at least seven years before this tragedy, and I will address myself in a few moments to what he did as a prisoner in those seven years, but to call him an ordinary boy, an ordinary man, an all American boy, is silly.

. . .

I don't want to get enmeshed in labels. I really want to talk about the personality characteristics that we all lay people understand and we have already delved into the isolation of the defendant starting in his high school years, going on through college and by the time he was a sophomore in college he had actually moved off campus and started to live a solitary life, which solitary life he lived through the fall of 1980. . . .

I don't believe I need to track Mr. Hinckley's very disconnected college career—it was a semester here, a semester out—but I do think it is important to focus on [several points] in that career. First is the spring of 1976 when John Hinckley impulsively [goes] out, abruptly sells his automobile and goes to California to become a rock star or a song writer. Unrealistic, absolutely unrealistic. He had not had one moment of training in music.

And he believed he would come on the front of Hollywood and be an instant success. Needless to say, he was a total failure and it resulted in his depression, despair, and disappointment.

He made another aborted effort, I believe in 1978, where the doctors testified he went to Nashville again with great expectations of being a rock star.

Once again his hopes were dashed, because, obviously, these were unrealistic goals.

Whether at that point in time they are psychotic, obviously we are not qualified to address that.

You should consider that, though, in your deliberations. . . .

He lives in a world where the only reality is that which he makes for himself. That which he defines for himself. His only experiences in the outside world as we think of it are things like eating, for instance, eating food. Ultimately travel.

That's not contact with the real world. That is not being exposed to the checks and balances we all need in our everyday lives, to know that we are making sense in our activities.

He had no such checks. The only checks he had were those that he had built up in his mind. It is in this period in 1979 that John Hinckley purchases his first weapon, I believe in August.

I point out—I should go back a moment to 1976, briefly, and recall to your mind that it was in that period when he was alone in Hollywood, alone in Hollywood, that he saw the movie "Taxi Driver," and he made identification, sympathized with Travis Bickle. I can't quite call him a hero. You saw the movie. Characterize him as you will.

But John Hinckley saw him as a loner, as he, Hinckley, was a loner. Isolated. Angry at what he saw in the outside world. Unable to establish any relationship in that world that he saw.

In 1979, you do see definite signs of mental disturbance, not just the purchase of the gun, but also you may remember in November 1979 a draft of a letter to his parents which was never sent.

Mr. Adelman this morning urged you to read that letter as an example of Mr. Hinckley's exploitiveness or—what shall we think of, the word to use?—entitlement. His sense of entitlement.

I think more important is to look at it and to observe how it reveals the defendant's self-image.

He is almost paralyzed. In fact, as the record shows, he ultimately is so paralyzed during the holidays of 1979 he can't even go home. He can't face his family in 1979, he is in such a state of depression.

Indeed, as Dr. Carpenter testified, in that period of 1979, the fall, he had suicidal ideas to the extent that he played Russian roulette on a number of occasions.

I'll admit that is self-reported. But that is all we have here.

[This idea] is confirmed by the existence of the photograph which is in evidence and which you will have available to you in your jury deliberations, which shows a very, very distressing picture of the defendant with a gun to his head. Much in the likeness of the character Travis Bickle from "Taxi Driver."

It is a sorry image. A sorry self-image, if you will, that this defendant photographed of himself in late '79 or early 1980.

In 1980 we know that the defendant's somatic complaints increased to such a point that his parents became concerned and brought him home and had him checked [by local doctors].

The Government seizes right away the fact that [these doctors] observed no mental problem with the defendant.

Ladies and gentlemen of the jury, I submit to you that the mental problem that the defendant was suffering from by the end of 1979 and by early 1980 was so deep, so deeply rooted in himself that it would take hours and hours of psychiatric examination to ferret it out.

Something far beyond the capacity of a medical doctor to do.

I think the only observation which is reported in this regard, I think, is the notation in one of the medical records that the defendant's weight at that point in time, I believe in February of 1980, was 230 pounds.

The earlier Texas Tech records, clinical records, taken some several years before, shows him to be 165, 170 pounds. An extraordinary gain of weight. An extraordinary gain of weight.

We all know that the defendant became aware of Jodie Foster attending Yale in May of 1980.

We have heard testimony that he became fascinated and enchanted with Miss Foster and starting in 1976, with the movie Taxi Driver. When he saw in 1980 that she was in Yale, he lives in a world, builds a new goal. And Miss Foster becomes the focus of the defendant's attentions.

You all know in August the defendant returns home and was examined by [his father's] company psychiatrist, who urged the family to adopt some type of plan for the defendant so he had goals so he could see today where he is going to be next year or next month.

That results in what I suggest is a manipulative effort of the defendant to get money from his family so he can go and establish a relationship up through and including March 30, 1981 . . . .

In any event, the defendant goes to New Haven, and, as you can reasonably expect, there is no relationship. No real relationship to be established with Miss Foster.

And in reaction to that, I don't think a realistic reaction, but in reaction to that the defendant is angry. He is distressed.

Again, the identification with the film "Taxi Driver," he thinks of a way to remedy this.

His remedy then becomes to stalk President Carter, which he does on several occasions in October of 1980.

And, as you know, he changes his focus of that stalking to President Reagan following the election in November.

Again, I suggest the ideation, the thought, that by stalking the President of the United States, he could in some way establish a relationship with the young woman, is bizarre.

I submit to you that it is a result of a serious mental illness in which the defendant's relation to reality in the true meaningful sense has been severed, has been impaired.

I suggest that the impairment continues in the months following September and through the whole fall of 1980.

Ultimately it leads to frustration on the part of the defendant and leads him to his home in Evergreen in October when he attempts suicide by taking [a drug] overdose....

This act, of course, results in the parents referring the defendant to [a local psychiatrist], Dr. Hopper....

I suggest to you that the entire relationship with Dr. Hopper was an unfortunate one. I don't blame Dr. Hopper. I don't blame the defendant.

I say to you that at that point in time, in October of 1980, this defendant's mental condition had deteriorated to such a state that he was unable to communicate his innermost thoughts to anyone.

The slight effort he made, he gave a signal. He gave a written signal to Dr. Hopper that he was obsessed "with the woman I referred to last week."

Jodie Foster.

And I think, through no fault of Dr. Hopper's he thought that was simply a young man's fancy with a movie actress.

I do not believe he had the slightest appreciation of the seriousness and the intensity of John Hinckley's involvement with Jodie Foster and John Hinckley's unreal expectation that he would one day have a relationship with Jodie Foster.

I think the failure of the defendant to reveal his activities through the months of October, November, December, and January, to Dr. Hopper are a reflection of Mr. Hinckley's inability to communicate.

I think it is unfortunate that Dr. Hopper didn't pursue John Hinckley's whereabouts when he missed appointments, but apparently that wasn't done.

I don't know that it would have done any good, but it didn't happen.

Another impediment to there being any meaningful relationship between this defendant and Dr. Hopper was the fact that Dr. Hopper was talking to the defendant's parents. Not that he was giving them therapy, but Dr. Hopper I believe in efforts to help the defendant thought it might be useful to get insight from his parents.

But what was the result? The defendant sees this as Dr. Hopper being simply a conduit of information from him, John Hinckley, through Dr. Hopper, back to his parents.

And he does not want his parents to know what he is up to because he knows that were he to reveal to his parents that he had been stalking

President Carter, that he had been stalking anybody, that his parents would have taken swift and severe action, so the defendant wouldn't tell him. The defendant wouldn't tell him anything.

That is not evidence of appreciation of wrongfulness. That is not evidence of ability to control or conform your conduct to the requirements of the law.

The defendant's actions are the actions of a psychotic who had a fear that he was sick, and like many ill people afraid to reveal it for fear of the consequences. . . .

[A] very significant piece of evidence . . . is the New Year's monologue of 1981.

This is Mr. Hinckley speaking to a tape recorder:

"John Lennon is dead. The world is over. Forget it. . . . It's just gonna be insanity, if I even make it through the first few days. . . . I still regret having to go on with 1981 . . . I don't know why people wanna live.

"John Lennon is dead. . . . I still think—I still think about Jodie all the time. That's all I think about really. That, and John Lennon's death. They were sorta binded together. . . .

"I hate New Haven with a mortal passion. I've been up there many times, not stalking her really, but just looking after her. . . . I was going to take her away for a while there, but I don't know. I am so sick I can't even do that. . . . It'll be total suicide city. I mean, I couldn't care less. Jodie is the only thing that matters now. Anything I might do in 1981 would be solely for Jodie Foster's sake.

"My obsession is Jodie Foster. . . . I've gotta, I've gotta find her and talk to her some way in person or something. . . . That's all I want her to know, is that I love her. I don't want to hurt her. . . . I think I'd rather just see her not, not on earth, than being with other guys. . . . I wouldn't want to stay here on earth without her.

That is not exhaustive, but it is representative, I believe, of the thinking of the defendant at that time. I think it reflects a very disturbed state of mind, a state of mind which is totally detached from reality.

And unfortunately there is no one to check, no one to test that reality with John Hinckley.

Again, while he is at home, he is alone. You may remember, in fact, I think, at the Christmas holidays that year his family described his situation at a dinner table when he simply hung his head and was almost limp for a period of minutes and got up and left the table.

He hadn't communicated with his own family.

[You] can track very closely the defendant's travel through the months of the early fall and winter of 1981. And I think these are all consistent with what I am suggesting to you now, that the defendant's motivating, driving forces are unreal, that [there has been] detachment from reality as you and I know it to be.

There develops, or starts to develop, now in January of 1981 a new crisis in the defendant Hinckley's life. [A] plan is devised between the Hinckleys, including the defendant, and Dr. Hopper to set certain goals for the defendant.

I believe the goal was [that by] March 1 [he was] to have a job and by the end of March be out of the house.

Now, if you look at the history of the defendant up to that point in time, his behavior is so erratic and so impulsive and so unpredictable that it is quite apparent to us today that he is unable to hold a job.

And the goals that were set up for him were impossible for him externally, and an unrealistic goal. Insofar as he could understand it, he knew he could not live with it.

There was no way that this defendant could become gainfully employed and self-sufficient in the time-frame allowed to him. And it is during this period of January and February of 1981, when we go through this incredible process of homicide/suicide/murder, these are bizarre thoughts.

To what end? To gain the love and admiration and establish a relationship with a woman. It is delusional thinking. That's all it is, pure and simple. It is pathetic, but it is delusional.

You know that the last week of February his parents were away, and on March 1 when they returned they had a note on their door which says "Your prodigal son has left again. I must exorcise some demons" or something to that effect.

Once again the defendant departs. He goes to New Haven. And he leaves a series of communications with Jodie Foster.

They are bizarre. "I love you six trillion times. Wait for me. I will rescue you."

In fact, these notes were so disturbing to Jodie Foster—you saw a videotape of her—that she turned those notes over to her dean. She was so concerned. These were bizarre thoughts that were being expressed to her.

Of course, then we know the defendant returns to New York without funds and he calls his parents in desperation. [During] Park Dietz's interview of the defendant, he said, "I never expected to need any money when I went to New York in March because I thought I would be dead or in jail."

Well, he was not. He had no money. He called his parents in desperation and he was shocked to learn that they would not just welcome him back. They were distressed.

They put him off. . . .

[On] the advice of Dr. Hopper [they] were going to make him sweat it out a little bit, to see if this wouldn't make him shape up.

[They] relented and they arranged for Mr. Hinckley to return to Evergreen [the family home].

Well, he did indeed return to Evergreen and he arrived there on [March] 7th. He was met at the airport that evening by his father. Bear in mind his depression at that time and consider the shock, the disbelief, the utter wonderment that Mr. Hinckley experienced when his father told him "You can't come home, John. We have had it."

In making this decision I by no means am critical of the parents. I don't think the blame can be laid at anybody's feet. I think they acted in good faith. They relied in good faith upon what they believed was psychiatric expertise. [The] psychiatrist was unable to probe into the depths of this defendant's mind to understand the severity of the illness with which he was afflicted, so the advice Dr. Hopper gave and the advice the parents accepted seemed reasonable to all concerned except to the defendant Hinckley.

[Dr. Carpenter] suggested that when Mr. Hinckley was told by his father you can't come home, that was the severance of his last anchor to reality.

Bear in mind that for many years the only ties he had to reality were occasional, perhaps yearly, visits with his parents. Now on [March] 7, 1981, he is without any anchor.

As we know, he moved to the motel, [and] lived there for approximately two weeks, again in isolation. However, this period of isolation, I suggest to you, is a little different than the prior seven years of total isolation. I described those seven years as "total isolation."

I can only describe this as being more isolated than he ever experienced. Fortunately or unfortunately, as the case may be, Mrs. Hinckley as a mother was not able perhaps to adhere to the plan with the same rigidity that the father could, so the defendant was able during those two weeks to visit his mother on a few occasions at her home in Evergreen, but the handwriting was clear. The writing on the wall was clear. He has to move on.

He was not getting any more support from his family. He sold his guitar, he sold his records, he sold his typewriter. He sold guns.

And you reflect for the moment on those hours. It was an hour or an hour-and-a-half drive to the airport on March 24th when the defendant had imposed upon his mother and implored with her to drive him to the airport, and hour and a half of stony silence between the mother and her son.

I said a moment ago the last anchor was ended on [March] 7th. I suggest the last anchor was really severed on March 24th and he is then cut adrift without any resources, with no resources to do anything for himself except that he has money. He could buy his clothing, he can buy his food, he can find shelter, he can travel. But he has no hope, no future and what does he resort to?

He resorts to more fantasy thinking. "What am I to do? My life is at an end."

And we have heard testimony what his options were. We have heard testimony he thought "I had better go back to New Haven and shoot myself in front of Jodie Foster, or shoot her and shoot myself."

And indeed the testimony is that when he embarked toward the East Coast on March 25th, that is where he was headed.

. . .

[Mr. Adelman] seemed to argue that you could not infer that the defendant was in a psychotic condition because he was not conducting himself in an open and obviously bizarre fashion.

I think the evidence is clear from both sides, both experts, all experts, that the ability of a schizophrenic to maintain a contact with common reality is not unusual, that is to say, a severely ill psychotic schizophrenic inside may have a world of troubles unnoticed totally, unnoticed by us laymen, and bizarre conduct is not an indispensable ingredient to a diagnosis of schizophrenia.

Indeed, Mr. Adelman suggested that one of our doctors described Mr. Hinckley as being in a frenzy. What we said was he was in an internal frenzy. Mr. Adelman suggested to you yesterday had he been in a frenzy, he would be stumbling on the floor and not drinking a coke in the Park Central Hotel on the morning before the shooting.

I suggest to you that is misleading. The kind of frenzy that we are talking about is an internal frenzy, an internal confusion, one that is going on in this man's inner world, all built upon false premises, false assumptions, false ideas.

At one point, I believe in his opening statement, Mr. Adelman suggested psychiatric influences, thought delusions, fantasies are not evidence you should consider in this case. That is precisely the evidence you should consider in this case. That is why we are here. . . .

Again Mr. Adelman yesterday suggested that we had offered to you a smorgasbord of insanity and he alluded to "Taxi Driver," [Hinckley's poems], Jodie Foster, sleep deprivation, the CAT-scan.

Ladies and gentlemen, this is evidence. This is probative evidence going to the condition of this defendant's state of mind and please don't be misled by a characterization that the evidence we have offered to you of this defendant's state of mind is a smorgasbord.

. . .

I submit to you that it is not possible to reconstruct, as the Government physicians have tried to do, the minute-by-minute progression of the defendant's thought processes from the moment he left the Hilton until the moment he shot the President and the three other innocent victims.

For any of us to reflect back some moment in time and try to attempt to think what we were thinking is almost an impossible task. And I suggest to you that the efforts of the psychiatrists to build the moment-by-moment thoughts that Mr. Hinckley was entertaining in those moments, half-hour between the time he arrived at the Hilton and the time he actually did the shooting is impossible.

I suggest to you that the entire time that Mr. Hinckley was at the Hilton, the moment he saw the President, when he arrived, he was in such a deluded state he knew if you asked him "It is right to shoot the President?" Undoubtedly he would say "You don't shoot people."

But in his delusion, he is not aware of the humanity of those victims. They play a very minor role in his delusional state. They are merely means to the end, to the end he wishes to accomplish: To win the love and affection and establish the relationship with Jodie Foster.

I remind you that even Dr. Dietz stated that these were not the reasonable acts of a completely rational individual. I suggest to you that is a gross understatement of Mr. Hinckley's condition at that time.

Now, summing up Dr. Carpenter's [testimony], he described the defendant's suicidal thoughts going back as early as 1976. . . .

[In 1979 the defendant] purchases a gun and later plays Russian Roulette. Dr. Carpenter alludes to the photographs with the gun to the head. He talks about the overdose of Surmontil. These are all evidences of suicide. Evidence of this defendant's depression that existed during this critical period of time.

The delusions I've described, the ideas of reference I've described, the blunted affect I've described and, again, I remind you the blunted affect really is a flatness in the emotional content of the individual. That is significant when you come to consider the totality of Mr. Hinckley's ability to appreciate the wrongfulness of his conduct. . . .

Dr. Carpenter was meticulous in reviewing the entire historical buildup to that moment of stress, of ultimate stress on March 30, 1981.

Those are the factors that were considered and should be considered by you and were considered by Dr. Carpenter in assessing the defendant's responsibility.

And when asked, Dr. Carpenter said that in his opinion, the defendant, as a result of mental disease at the time of the shooting, lacked substantial capacity to conform his conduct to the requirements of the law.

He suggested at that point while he may have known intellectually—at a very superficial intellectual level—[that] it is wrong to shoot Presidents or anybody else, he was then dominated by his inner state, his inner self, his psychotic delusions.

And he was so involved in this commitment to this woman, Jodie Foster, that nothing else mattered but that he achieve his goal.

Again, I think his characterization of the victims' tragedy, though it may be as bit players, they were bit players in the mind of the defendant.

I do not suggest to you that they are bit players to any of us because, indeed, they are not. But in his delusional state, that's what they were.

Likewise, when asked, Dr. Carpenter testified that the defendant lacked the substantial capacity to appreciate the wrongfulness of his conduct of March 30. And again, he talked about intellectual quality in a poor superficial thinking level the defendant would have known it was wrong. But when viewing "appreciate" as connoting something more than just intellectual awareness, but a quality of reason, the reasoning process has not just intellectual components but emotional components. The reasoning process was so impaired that the defendant was unable to appreciate wrongfulness of his conduct. That is the testimony of Dr. Carpenter.

In his own mind the defendant had two compelling reasons to do what he did. To terminate his own existence and to accomplish his ideal union with Jodie Foster, whether it be in this world or the next.

.   .   .

[In] a classic understatement, Dr. Dietz stated that these were not the reasonable acts of a completely rational individual.

I submit these are the acts of a totally irrational individual, driven and motivated by his own world which he created for himself, locked in his own mind, without any opportunity to have any test of those ideas from the real world because of his total isolation.

Now, I want you to consider in summary form the stress factors that were building up in the period before the shooting.

Obviously the first stress factor was the failure of the defendant to establish a relationship with Jodie Foster.

A second stress factor was the death of John Lennon in December of 1980.

I remind you of the monologue of New Year's Eve and ask you to consider playing that. Hear once again the kind of distress and bizarre thinking that the defendant was expressing at that time.

I think a very significant stress factor in this defendant's life in this period was the failure of the psychiatric treatment.

Again I don't blame anybody. I only blame the defendant's mental illness because of his inability to verbalize what was going on in his mind. Whether it was some internal inability or fear of disclosure to his parents, or just fear, I don't know. But he did not disclose to his psychiatrist what was going on. And he experienced, in that, failure—the psychiatric therapy was doing him no good.

Another stress factor that I think is significant, is one I alluded to this morning, is that event of March 6, when he was in New York, stranded, without funds, wanting to come home, and rejected.

Another factor, of course, is March 7, when he arrives home and receives the ultimate, ultimate insult to him, that he is no longer welcome in the Hinckley household.

And I add to that, that very tragic and emotional moment in the defendant's life when his mother said goodbye at the airport, with a note of finality—not in the mother's mind, but in the defendant's mind.

Now, stress factors have a significance to this case that you must bear in mind.

Dr. Dietz agreed that under periods of extreme stress, transient psychotic symptoms may be present in the mental disorders which he admitted the defendant suffered from. And I submit to you that the stress, accepting the Government's analysis of the mental disorder, the mental disease, I submit to you that the stresses that had built up in this man through the end of March of 1980 reached psychotic proportions.

I submit to you that this evidence demonstrates the Government has failed in its burden of proving that this defendant was mentally responsible, that this defendant had the capacity to appreciate the wrongfulness of his conduct on March 30, 1981, that this defendant was able to conform his conduct to the requirements of the law.

I submit the Government has failed to meet that burden.

Rebuttal by Mr. Adelman

We didn't go through six weeks of trial to have a lawyer stand up here and tell you to forget about what happened.

We didn't go through six weeks of trial to have a lawyer stand up here for two and one-half hours and not make one mention of the charges in this indictment. Did we?

Your sworn, your sworn duty is to deal with the evidence.

And no lawyer can talk you out of that.

No lawyer can make you go run away.

[T]he best they can produce is what the argument he gave today and yesterday was. That is it. That is the evidence.

That is the best they can do.

Now let me go back and talk [about March 30]. He avoided March 30 like the plague. I timed it. He took exactly six minutes, of all that talk, to talk about March 30 and the reasons [Hinckley] could not appreciate the wrongfulness of his act.

That is no accident. Mr. Fuller knows his business, and Mr. Fuller knows he can't deal with the facts and the evidence of March 30. Can he?

How outrageous to say to you that nobody can reconstruct Mr. Hinckley's thoughts of March 30, 1981, like the Government doctors did.

How did they do it? By talking to him and recording what he said. The doctors didn't make up these thoughts.

John Hinckley told them, for goodness' sake....

The reason Mr. Fuller wants you to put aside the events of March 30 [is] because, indeed, they are so meaningful.

Indeed, they mean something in this case.

They are the foundation for these charges. They are the foundations for [the conclusion] that Mr. Hinckley, indeed, as the evidence shows, is criminally responsible.

What is the evidence he wants you to put aside?

The gun. Who brought the gun to Washington? John Hinckley.

The Devastator bullets. Who brought them to Washington? John Hinckley.

Who purchased six Devastator bullets? Take a look at the box when you are back there. There are twelve holes in the box and only six bullets were brought to Washington. Who brought those? John Hinckley.

"Forget about it," said Mr. Fuller.

John Hinckley would like to go under that table right now, but he can't do that.

We are in a court of law, and twelve of you are going to decide his fate.

Forget about the victims. Forget about Mr. McCarthy, Mr. Delahanty, Mr. Reagan, and Mr. Brady.

Go ahead. Forget about them.

Simply by conceding, as the defense so grandly does, that Mr. Hinckley was stalking and running around in the fall of 1980, that you are supposed to forget about that, too.

What are the issues here? You wouldn't know after you heard Mr. Fuller talk.

The questions of criminal responsibility have two parts. He tap danced around in Part 1 for that matter. He didn't say anything about Part 2 and, of course, I told you quite a bit about that, and when we go on I will talk further.

He gave you no reasons. Remember, he was talking for the first few minutes there about reasons he was going to give. He gave you no reason whatsoever to question, to doubt, if you will, any of the testimony Dr. Johnson, Dr. Dietz and, indeed, some of the defense doctors about Mr. Hinckley's ability to appreciate wrongfulness and conform behavior to the requirements of law.

Let's get it straight. We never contended—because we can't and because the evidence doesn't permit it—that Mr. Hinckley didn't have a mental disorder on March 30th. He sure did. He had personality disorders and he had, as the Government team said, mood disorders or dysthymic disorders.

He was a sad, depressed person. We never contended otherwise, but the critical question is did that impair his ability to appreciate wrongfulness and conform behavior? And the evidence is clear and unrebutted by counsel that it did not. That is the critical point.

What you have had here in the defense argument is what I might call a parade of irrelevancies. What did we hear over the last four or five hours of this argument? About his 1976 trip to California. Trip to Nashville. Blunted affect for goodness sake? Blunted affect isn't in DSM–III as a mental disorder. . . .

Mark Chapman.[j] How Dr. Dietz takes notes. These are the irrelevancies that counsel has had to bring forth here. John Lennon. That poem about John Lennon. The New Year's Eve monologue three months before the crime.

Remember, I told you. Remember, that is a good point. Remember, I told you that everything I said was going to be anchored back to March 30th. I was going to tell you how it related to March 30th.

[The] Court will tell you in instructions . . . that evidence about Mr. Hinckley's mental condition before and after [March 30] is admissible and relevant to the extent it relates to his mental condition and criminal responsibility at the time of the crime.

We are not trying John Hinckley as to how his mental condition was in 1980 at Christmastime when he is sitting around looking out the

j Chapman killed John Lennon. [Footnote by eds.]

window and so forth. We are not trying that. We are not trying his mental condition on New Year's Eve.

I think if we tried a lot of people's mental condition on New Year's Eve, it might be similar to John Hinckley on that date.

We are trying March 30, 1981.

[Defense counsel] is telling us, for instance, that John Hinckley wouldn't play his guitar in front of his parents. That is 1972. That shows that this man can't conform his behavior to the requirements of the law?

Really, you see the defense strategy in this case and we have seen it right clear here, is to sweep away, to ignore, to hide, . . . to do away with what they can't deal with.

Let's cite a good example of that, the lay witnesses.

Mr. Fuller says, "Well, you can't believe these people. They only saw Mr. Hinckley for a few brief minutes."

That is not true. Mrs. Kondeah [the maid at the Park Central] did, sure. But the significance of Mrs. Kondeah is not what Mr. Hinckley said to her. It is what he didn't do, what he didn't say.

If he is psychotic, despite what Mr. Fuller says, the evidence shows [that] a psychotic person will reveal that behavior.

Mrs. Kondeah doesn't see anything unusual. She said he was calm. "Calm" doesn't appear in DSM–III. That is her common sense way of expressing things.

Danny Spriggs [the Secret Service agent who apprehended Hinckley] likewise. Sure, he only heard four words from Mr. Hinckley. Again he wasn't put on to probe his inner thought process, but he was put on to explain from his experience. Remember, he had some training in the Secret Service on mental matters. From his experience he didn't see anything wrong and disordered with Mr. Hinckley.

Oh, we go to Eddie Myers, the policeman. Eddie Myers reports a lot of things about Mr. Hinckley. He didn't say he was depressed. He didn't say he was sleepy.

[FBI] Agent Aquilia talked a long time with Mr. Hinckley off and on about the common things. The basketball game, the Academy Awards, and things of that character. He didn't say he was depressed. . . .

Now those are details. Those are evidence and those are facts. We don't hear them from counsel. And maybe you can understand why.

I have to represent this about John Hinckley and you have to deal with the testimony of these people. These lay witnesses together as a group saw Mr. Hinckley for eight hours, I believe, from 1:15 all the way up to 10 o'clock. There was an hour break in there for the shooting and the important fact is that these witnesses don't know each other, as I made clear to you earlier, but they all report the same thing.

He is not sleepy. He is not high. He is not depressed. He is coherent. He is talking.

Now this is a man who counsel claims is psychotic, inner world or what-have-you. No way. He just can't be.

Counsel would have you believe that there is a battle of psychiatrists going on here. I say there really is no battle. There really is no battle! We are talking about psychiatrists who operate on different levels.

Dr. Johnson and Dr. Dietz find out the facts and the evidence and apply it to the case and apply it to the indictment and apply it to the evidence. . . .

When you apply all of this knowledge to the facts, the informational knowledge, you see Mr. Hinckley sure did have the ability to appreciate and conform, so there is no battle of the psychiatrists at all.

The lay witnesses make it clear Mr. Hinckley had the ability to conform, appreciate and indeed, ladies and gentlemen, you might even think if Dr. Carpenter [and the other defense experts] had done their homework like Dr. Dietz and his team and Dr. Johnson and her team, they might even come to the same conclusion.

There is no battle here at all.

Let me talk about a couple of other points Mr. Fuller makes.

The Government psychiatrist, he says, trivialized—that is his word—the "frenetic behavior of the defendant." What frenetic behavior? Yeah, he flew all over the place. He flew on United Airlines. That is not the behavior of a frenetic man. That is the behavior of a desperate, bored young man with a pocket full of money, who got from his parents $3600, who likes Jodie Foster. Wouldn't we all like to be in that situation? Fly to California or wherever?

He had the opportunity. He had the time. He had the means. That is not a sign or symptom of mental disorder. And it is really unfair for Mr. Fuller to say the Government doctors trivialized this. They say, indeed, that Mr. Hinckley was depressed, that he was lonely and that was a sign of his personality disorders and his dysthymic disorders.

Likewise, Mr. Fuller says, "For goodness sake, the Government doctor could see normalcy between Mr. Hinckley and his parents." Dr. Dietz said that all along Mr. Hinckley didn't get along with his parents, particularly his father.

In fact, Mr. Hinckley told Dr. Hopper—Dr. Hopper now—that he didn't want to work. He would rather be a writer and get his inheritance. That is why they didn't get along, because his parents, like good parents would and should, wanted him to get out and work, and he wouldn't do that.

The Government doctors took that into account. The Government doctors reported that. . . .

One of the reasons Dr. Dietz assigned for the events of March 30th is Mr. Hinckley's lack of success in job-seeking, lack of success in dealing with his parents. Mr. Fuller is certainly wrong when he said that the only reason Mr. Hinckley did the shooting was to impress Miss Foster.

Dr. Johnson, Dr. Dietz testified to a host of reasons and that was just one ... but make no mistakes about it, ladies and gentlemen. Try as you might, Mr. Fuller can't run away from the evidence. He can't run away from the evidence.

. . .

Ladies and gentlemen, of all the writings introduced in this case, all the writings introduced in this case, there is only one that tells you what John Hinckley's mind was like on March 30, 1981. The reason for that is simple. All the other writings were months, weeks, days, years before. Some of them, 1976, as I recall.

And Dr. Dietz told us that you can't even tell a person's state of mind from poems because they are fiction, and Mr. Fuller couldn't wrestle with that one, because I'm sure he realizes it is true. Poetry is fiction. As I say, only one writing speaks about the state of mind of John Hinckley on March 30, 1981, that is the "Jodie" letter.

Dr. Johnson analyzed the "Jodie" letter and she talked to Mr. Hinckley about it. What did she tell you? She said it tells how Mr. Hinckley is able to appreciate wrongfulness and conform his behavior. We went through that with you yesterday.

You didn't hear defense say anything. She went through it and line one, he writes: "There is a definite possibility I'll be killed in my attempt to get Reagan."

Appreciation of wrongfulness, certainly.

Ability to conform behavior, unquestionably.

Other discussions in here about "this historical deed," doesn't he recognize by that alone, it is appreciation of wrongfulness and ability to conform behavior?

. . .

All the other doctors who testified, the Government doctors indicated quite clearly Mr. Hinckley appreciated the wrongfulness. I certainly don't have to go through all the testimony for you. The rule of law is whether he could appreciate. Period.

There is no division, modification, or anything of that sort on the word appreciate. Isn't it clear from the Jodie Foster letter alone, the Jodie letter alone, Mr. Hinckley appreciated the wrongfulness of what he is doing?

From all the background, Mr. Hinckley stalking all through the fall and in the winter, Mr. Hinckley target practicing. Doesn't he appreciate all of this is wrong and my goodness, having read about all the assassinations all the way back to J.F.K., didn't he appreciate it is wrong?

How can counsel argue to you otherwise? [This] is a man who counsel claims doesn't appreciate deep down the wrongfulness of the crime [yet who said at the time of the crime] "Should I, Should I?" That is appreciation. From him.

Here is a man who said, "I'm not that desperate. I might go home because of the rain. I'm not that desperate." Doesn't he appreciate the wrongfulness of all that is going on? Here is a man at the time of the crime four days, five days later, told Dr. Johnson ... "This is the best opportunity I'll have."

Without question, that is deep down appreciation of what is wrong about this conduct and that it is wrong. You see, there is no argument here from the defense because there cannot be, there simply can't be.

Now, Mr. Fuller said, and remember, I told you earlier in the hour Mr. Fuller said John Hinckley shot President Reagan to impress Jodie Foster. That is flat wrong. . . .

Mr. Hinckley had many purposes. [One is that he] wanted to achieve notoriety and fame.

What does all this mean? It means John Hinckley is a narcissistic personality. He wants attention. It doesn't mean he has a serious mental disorder. It does not mean he cannot appreciate wrongfulness of his conduct.

It further was said, the testimony was from both doctors, that John Hinckley wanted to prove himself, as [Dr. Johnson] put it, sub-consciously. Dr. Dietz said, "This is in reaction to the ultimatum from his parents."

"Prove himself." Here is John Hinckley, the fifth wheel in that family. John Hinckley, the black sheep. One way or another he is going to make his mark and he decided he would. We can say that is a dumb way. Being stupid is not a mental disorder. It is not in that book.

Doing things for a foolish reason is not a mental disorder. It is just can he appreciate wrongfulness? Can he conform behavior? John Hinckley sure could. John Hinckley sure could.

In addition, Dr. Johnson said furthermore, another reason is to get back at all those people who had let him down in the past. Here, his parents again. . . .

So you see, we have many, many reasons; many, many goals besides the concern with Jodie Foster.

In fact, if you really think about it, it is a secondary reason. . . .

Mr. Fuller also said [his] parents gave an ultimatum. Get out of the house. This set John Hinckley off. John Hinckley was a hunter, a stalker, before March 7, 1981. He brought a gun to Nashville, to Dayton. He showed up in Washington looking for President Reagan. Hunting and stalking, you see.

That is John Hinckley. That is what he was until the time of this crime.

Now we are told by Mr. Fuller, in his argument, the victims of this crime are bit players in John Hinckley's troubled mind. I wish the victims were here to hear that, that they are bit players in this young man's mind. It is not a troubled mind, it is a depressed mind, a sad mind, not a troubled mind.

It would be nice if Jim Brady could hear this morning that he is a bit player. It would be nice if Tim McCarthy and Tom Delahanty and President Reagan could hear that they are bit players in John Hinckley's mind. . . .

And it would also be nice, as I said before, very interesting, if Jim Brady were told today the lawyer for John Hinckley said forget about the Devastator bullets. Go ahead Jim Brady. Forget about it! Just imagine! Just imagine!

And think of the audacity of that argument. And as long as you deliberate, think of the audacity of that argument.

Dr. Johnson, as in so many situations in her case, hit her nail right on the head. And you can recall she said one of the characteristics of John Hinckley's personality was to put the blame on everybody else.

And that in talking to him and learning about him, as she did, Mr. Hinckley put the blame for what happened on March 30 on his parents, on the Secret Service for not protecting the President properly. On Dr. Hopper. On Jodie Foster. On "Taxi Driver."

Jodie Foster didn't take the Devastator bullets and shoot the victims. The Secret Service didn't shoot Jim Brady. John Hopper didn't shoot anybody.

Mr. and Mrs. Hinckley didn't shoot anybody. John Hinckley did. You see. What I'm telling you and what we said and what we have done here in this case, what I'm going to ask you to do when you return guilty verdicts, is to recognize through those verdicts the time has come for John Hinckley, Jr., for the first time in his life, to take responsibility for what he has done.

John Hinckley, for 26 years, has avoided responsibility in every corner of his life. But John Hinckley, I say to you, based on this evidence, cannot avoid the responsibility for what he did on March 30, 1981. He can't avoid the responsibility of shooting President Reagan.

And he can't avoid the responsibility of shooting Tom Delahanty in the back. And he can't avoid the responsibility of shooting Tim McCarthy and goodness, he can't avoid the responsibility of shooting Jim Brady in the head.

Ladies and gentlemen, I ask you, and I am only a representative of the Government and as the Government representative I ask you to do this: As in every case we ask you to do justice.

If you are tired of deliberating, look at the evidence and think about it and I suggest to you that justice in this case, taking into account everything I have said and all the evidence, is for you to return verdicts of guilty on each of the counts of this indictment and for you to find at the same time that John Hinckley is responsible for each of these counts in this indictment, and that John Hinckley for the first time in his life can stand up and be responsible because in this case that is justice.

I thank you.

4. Jury Instructions. After the closing argument the trial judge instructed the jury on the law applicable to the decision then to be made. Excerpts from these instructions follow.

Instructions by Judge Parker

The burden of proof in this, as in every other criminal proceeding, is placed upon the prosecution. Every defendant in a criminal proceeding is presumed to be innocent and this presumption of innocence is attached to the defendant throughout the trial until the defendant is proved guilty beyond a reasonable doubt.

The burden is on the prosecution to prove the defendant guilty beyond a reasonable doubt, and if the prosecution fails to sustain that burden then you have no alternative save to return a verdict of not guilty.

A defendant is not required under our system of jurisprudence to establish or to offer proof of innocence, but rather the responsibility is placed upon the shoulders of the prosecution. You are further instructed that the burden of proof never shifts or changes during the course of the trial.

Now, what does the Court mean in law by the concept of a reasonable doubt? It is a doubt based on reason, a doubt for which you can give a reason. It is not a fanciful doubt. It is not a whimsical doubt, nor a doubt based wholly on conjecture. The prosecution is not required to establish the guilt of a defendant beyond all doubt or guilt of a defendant to a mathematical or to a scientific certainty. Its burden is simply to establish guilt beyond a reasonable doubt. Now, perhaps this will assist you to better understand what the Court has in mind by reasonable doubt.

If after an impartial comparison and consideration of all of the evidence you can candidly say that you have such a doubt as would cause you to hesitate to act in matters of importance to you yourself, then you have a reasonable doubt. But if after such an impartial comparison and consideration of all of the evidence and giving due consideration to the presumption of innocence which attaches to the defendant, you can truthfully say that you have an abiding conviction of the defendant's guilt such as would not cause you to hesitate to act upon in the more weighty and more serious and important matters relating to your personal affairs, then you do not have a reasonable doubt.

Now the concept of reasonable doubt, which I have just alluded to, which I have just instructed you on, not only refers and applies to the substantive counts of the indictment, but also apply to the issue of criminal responsibility which I will develop later on.

. . .

An issue is presented in this case concerning the mental condition of the defendant on March 30, 1981, the date of the several offenses alleged in the 13–count indictment.

Now, in addition to proving beyond a reasonable doubt the elements of the 13 offenses charged in the indictment, the prosecution also has a burden of proving the defendant's criminal responsibility beyond a reasonable doubt.

If you find that the Government has failed to prove beyond a reasonable doubt any one or more of the essential elements of the offense, you must find the defendant not guilty, and you should not consider any possible verdict relating to the question of criminal responsibility or insanity.

If you find the Government has proved each essential element of the offense beyond a reasonable doubt, then you must consider whether to bring in a verdict of not guilty by reason of insanity.

And that leads me to instruct you as follows: That, with respect to each count, each of the 13 counts, of the indictment, there are three possible verdicts: guilty, not guilty, not guilty by reason of insanity.

And in that connection, the Court will afford you a jury verdict form which will indicate the act, the charge in the indictment, explain [i]n a summary fashion what it is, and to the right will give you the possible verdicts which I've just indicated: guilty, not guilty, or not guilty by reason of insanity.

The law provides that a jury shall bring in a verdict of not guilty by reason of insanity if at the time of the criminal conduct the defendant, as a result of mental disease or defect, either lacked substantial capacity to conform his conduct to the requirements of the law or lacked substantial capacity to appreciate the wrongfulness of his conduct.[k]

---

[k] After the evidence had been presented, the parties made further argument on the "appreciation" instruction. The basis for the argument was the instruction proposed by the court at the pretrial motions hearing. The government opposed this instruc-

Every man is presumed to be sane. That is, to be without mental disease or defect, and to be responsible for his acts.

But that presumption no longer controls when evidence is introduced that he may have a mental disease or defect.

The term "insanity" does not require a showing that the defendant was disoriented at the time or place.

"Mental disease or defect" includes any abnormal condition of the mind, regardless of its medical label, which substantially affects mental or emotional processes and substantially impairs his behavior controls.

The term "behavior controls" refers to the processes and capacity of a person to regulate and control his conduct and his actions.

In considering whether the defendant had a mental disease or defect at the time of the unlawful acts with which he is charged, you may consider testimony in this case concerning the development, adaptation, and functioning of these mental and emotional processes and behavior controls.

The term "mental disease" differs from "mental defect" in that the former is a condition which is either capable of improving or deteriorating, while the latter is a condition not capable of improving or deteriorating.

The burden is on the Government to prove beyond a reasonable doubt either that the defendant was not suffering from a mental disease or defect on March 30, 1981, or else that he nevertheless had substantial capacity on that date both to conform his conduct to the requirements of the law and to appreciate the wrongfulness of his conduct. If the Government has not established this to your satisfaction, beyond a reasonable doubt, then you shall bring a verdict of not guilty by reason of insanity.

In considering the issue of insanity, you may consider the evidence that has been admitted as to the defendant's mental condition before and after the several offenses charged, as well as the evidence as to the mental condition on that date, namely, March 30, 1981. The evidence as to the defendant's mental condition before and after that date was admitted solely for the purpose of assisting you to determine the defendant's condition on the date of the alleged offense, March 30, 1981.

You have heard the evidence of psychiatrists and a psychologist who testified as [expert witnesses]. An expert in a particular field, as I

tion because it left "open the question whether appreciate means cognitive, emotional or both." The government preferred to leave the term altogether undefined unless the court was willing to instruct the jury specifically that "appreciate" referred only to "cognitive or intellectual awareness or understanding." The defense, of course, preferred to refer expressly to emotional appreciation or at least to amplify the term as the court had proposed at the pretrial hearing. The court decided to leave the term undefined. [Footnote by eds.]

indicated, is permitted to give his opinion in evidence, and in this connection you are instructed that you are not bound by medical labels, definitions, or conclusions as to what is or is not a mental disease or defect. What psychiatrists and psychologists may or may not consider a mental disease or defect for clinical purposes where their concern is treatment may or may not be the same as mental disease or defect for the purposes of determining criminal responsibility. Whether the defendant had a mental disease or defect must be determined by you under the explanation of those terms as it was given to you by the Court.

There was also testimony of lay witnesses with respect to their observations of the defendant's appearance, behavior, speech and actions. Such persons are permitted to testify as to their own observations and other facts known to them and may express an opinion based upon those observations and facts known to them. In weighing the testimony of such lay witnesses you may consider the circumstances of each witness, his opportunity to observe the defendant and to know the facts to which he has testified, his willingness and capacity to expound freely as to his observations and knowledge, the basis for his opinion and conclusions, and the nearness or remoteness of his observations of the defendant in point of time to the commission of the offenses charged. You may also consider whether the witness observed extraordinary or bizarre acts performed by the defendant or whether the witness observed the defendant's conduct to be free of such extraordinary or bizarre acts.

In evaluating such testimony you should take into account the extent of the witness' observations of the defendant and the nature and length of time of the witness' contact with the defendant. You should bear in mind that an untrained person may not be readily able to detect mental disease or defect and that the failure of a lay witness to observe abnormal acts by the defendant may be significant only if the witness had prolonged and intimate contact with the defendant.

You are not bound by the opinions of either expert or lay witnesses and you should not arbitrarily or capriciously reject the testimony of any witness, but you should consider the testimony of each witness in connection with the other evidence in the case and give it such weight as you believe it is entitled to receive.

You may also consider that every man is presumed to be sane, that is, to be without mental disease or defect and to be responsible for his acts. You should consider this principle in light of all of the evidence in the case and give it such weight as you believe it is fairly entitled to receive.

You should consider the evidence with respect to the insanity or responsibility issue separately as to each offense with which the defendant is charged. If you find with reference to any offense that at the time of the criminal conduct with which the defendant is charged as a result of a mental disease or defect he either lacked substantial capacity to conform his conduct to the requirements of the law or lacked substantial capacity to appreciate the wrongfulness of his conduct, you must find the defendant "not guilty" of such offense "by reason of insanity."

In any event, this does not change the responsibility and burden placed upon the Government, namely, that it must prove beyond a reasonable doubt that the defendant was criminally responsible for his acts committed, allegedly committed on March 30, 1981.

If the defendant is found "not guilty by reason of insanity," it becomes the duty of the Court to commit him to St. Elizabeth's Hospital. There will be a hearing within 50 days to determine whether the defendant is entitled to be released. In that hearing the defendant has the burden of proof. The defendant will remain in custody and will be entitled to release from custody only if the Court finds by a preponderance of the evidence that he is not likely to injure himself or other persons due to a mental disease.

———

*

PART III

REACTIONS TO THE VERDICT

COMMENTS AND QUESTIONS ON THE *HINCKLEY* TRIAL

1. Public Reaction. The acquittal of John Hinckley shocked and angered the American public. Three days after the verdict, the New York Times referred to a "national reaction of stunned surprise" and a "cascade of public outrage." Most commentators were sharply critical: "an exercise in legal absurdity," said Russell Baker; "a travesty of justice," concluded James J. Kilpatrick; the trial, according to Tom Wicker, was a "dismaying spectacle"; Joseph Kraft thought the verdict "did violence to common sense."

What do you think? Should Hinckley have been convicted? If you had been a juror, how would you have voted? What were the critical issues, in your opinion, on which the verdict should have turned?

These questions pose a number of complex issues. And they lead to a number of possibilities, among them:

> One possibility is that the decision was right in all respects: that Hinckley should have been acquitted and that the law of insanity was both properly formulated in the court's instructions and properly applied to Hinckley by the jury.

> Another is that there was nothing wrong with the law as stated to the jury, but that the jury reached the wrong verdict on the evidence before it.

> Still another is that the jury reached the right verdict (or at least a defensible verdict) based on the law of insanity as it was stated by the court, but that the verdict was nonetheless wrong, although not the jury's fault, because a different law of insanity should have been used. If you think this is the case, the question then becomes in what respects the law of insanity should be modified.

Consider the following comments and questions as you think about whether one of these options—or yet another one—states the proper view of the case.

2. Mental Disease. As noted in the previous discussion of the history of the insanity defense, all tests for the defense require as a threshold condition that the defendant have suffered from a "mental disease or defect" at the time of the alleged criminal behavior. This requirement poses two separate problems in any case in which an insanity defense is raised. The first is legal: the law must determine the kinds of mental conditions that should be regarded as a "mental disease or defect" for this purpose. The second is factual: the jury must determine, based on the testimony it has heard, whether the defendant actually had one of the mental conditions that the law recognizes as a sufficient predicate for the defense.

(i) **The Legal Questions.** It is clear that the law regards a "psychotic" condition[a] as a sufficient "mental disease" under any formulation of the insanity defense. Indeed, psychosis is widely regarded as the *only* type of mental illness that is sufficient under the traditional *M'Naghten* formulation.[b] Recall, however, that the *McDonald* case defined "mental disease" for the District of Columbia insanity defense more broadly as "any abnormal condition of the mind which substantially affects mental or emotional processes and substantially impairs behavior controls."[c] It seems clear that this definition would encompass afflictions that no doctor would recognize as psychotic.

One of the legal issues presented by the *Hinckley* case is whether the concept of "mental disease" was properly defined by the law in the District of Columbia. The answer to this question significantly affects how far the insanity defense will be extended.

It is likely that most people who murder or who attempt murder could be found to have had some diagnosable disorder at the time of the act, particularly if given the kind of comprehensive clinical evaluation to which Hinckley was subjected. Indeed, virtually *anyone* who commits a violent crime is likely to have some type of diagnosable personality disorder. One of the imposing difficulties in determining the proper content of the insanity defense is how to distinguish the kinds of disorders that can serve as the predicate for a successful insanity defense from those that can not. The challenge is to identify the types of "mental disease" that count, without at the same time providing a basis for exonerating anyone who commits a crime.

Another way to think about this problem is to consider how the law can differentiate defects of character from defects of mental capacity.[d] The premise of the criminal law, in this view, is that most people who commit crimes are "bad." Their conduct results from a morally repug-

---

[a] Recall the medical definition of "psychotic" contained in DSM–IV, quoted in footnote r, page 20, above. The essential notion is that psychosis involves "gross impairment in reality-testing," often evidenced by hallucinations or delusions.

[b] See, e.g., Joseph Livermore and Paul Meehl, The Virtues of M'Naghten, 51 Minn. L.Rev. 789, 802–04 (1967); Robert Waelder, Psychiatry and the Problem of Criminal

Responsibility, 101 U.Pa.L.Rev. 378, 384 (1942).

[c] See page 21, above.

[d] Compare Parsons v. State, 81 Ala. 577, 594, 2 So. 854, 865 (1887): "A mere moral or emotional insanity, so-called, unconnected with disease of the mind, or irresistible impulse resulting from mere moral obliquity, or wicked propensities and habits, is not recognized as a defense to crime in our courts."

nant character deficiency that is not present in the general population of law-abiding citizens and that makes it proper to punish them for their crimes. From this perspective, the function of the insanity defense is to differentiate from these "ordinary" criminals the (presumably) small number who suffer from such gross mental disturbances that it is unfair to regard them as "bad." One question for the law is the role of the concept of "mental disease" in accomplishing this purpose.

It has been argued, however, that any effort to capture such distinctions by limiting the definition of mental disease is bound to be clinically oversimplified and morally arbitrary. It is said that psychological disorders do not come prepackaged in boxes labeled "severe" and "not severe," "mad" and "bad," "morally relevant" and "morally irrelevant." A narrow definition of mental disease limited to psychoses, the argument continues, arbitrarily excludes clinically profound psychological dysfunctions that could be morally significant in a given case. Only a broad definition of "mental disease" can properly capture the full range of morally relevant mental conditions.

How should the law define "mental disease"? Was the right definition used in the *Hinckley* case?

(ii) The Factual Questions. The *Hinckley* case also presents difficult factual questions. The defense psychiatrists insisted that Hinckley was psychotic. The government psychiatrists disagreed, although they admitted that Hinckley suffered from various personality disorders. Moreover, in its rebuttal to the defense attorney's closing argument, the government lawyer seemed to concede that Hinckley had a "mental disorder" at the time of the offense. Given these events, there are several positions the jury could have taken:

> One is that, given the broad legal definition of "mental disease" in the District of Columbia, the jury really had no choice but to find that Hinckley suffered from a qualifying "mental disease" at the time of the offense. Thus, on this view, the critical question may have been whether the remainder of the insanity test was satisfied.

> By contrast, it may be that the "mental disorders" admitted by the government and testified to by the government witnesses should not have been regarded as a "mental disease" within the *McDonald* definition. If the jury believed the government experts and disbelieved the defense experts, then it should have found that Hinckley did not have a qualifying "mental disease" and should therefore have convicted him. But was the jury given enough guidance in the court's instructions so that it realistically could have made such a determination?

> Finally, the jury could have believed the defense witnesses and disbelieved the government witnesses, concluding that Hinckley really was psychotic. If this was the conclusion, then Hinckley's guilt

would have turned on whether the remainder of the insanity defense was satisfied. Is this likely based on your reading of the testimony?

What view would you have taken on this matter if you had been on the jury?

3.   Appreciation of Wrongfulness. As developed at pages 12 and 19–20 above, the word "appreciate," as used in the first part of the Model Penal Code test, is ambiguous. On the one hand, it may refer to mere "cognitive" understanding. On this view, the issue is whether Hinckley would have given the right answer if asked just before he shot the President: "Do you understand that this is something you are not supposed to do? Do you understand that it is wrong to shoot Presidents?" It seems clear that Hinckley was sane under this standard.

Alternatively, the word "appreciate" may refer to a more "affective" understanding. On this view, the question was whether Hinckley had a full emotional appreciation of the significance and meaning of what he tried to do. Whether Hinckley was sane under this standard seems more problematical.

Judge Parker apparently ruled before the *Hinckley* trial that he would limit the word "appreciate" in the insanity formulation to the narrower "cognitive" meaning. Yet he permitted wide-ranging testimony by the defense experts exploring the extent to which Hinckley "appreciated" the wrongfulness of his act in the broader "affective" sense, and ultimately left the matter to the jury without clarifying instructions. Did Judge Parker handle this problem properly? If not, what should he have done? Perhaps more importantly, how should the law deal with this question in future cases?

4.   The Volitional Inquiry. The *Hinckley* case is a good illustration of the subtleties of the "volitional" or "control" part of the Model Penal Code test. On the one hand, it seems clear that Hinckley was less responsive than most persons to the influences that ordinarily deter unlawful behavior. He was a far cry from the "normal" son of affluent parents, and surely not quite the "ordinary person that has been put under a microscope" as depicted by the government lawyer in his closing argument.[e] It seems clear that Hinckley was emotionally disordered and that his decision to kill President Reagan was somehow connected with his disturbed condition.

Yet how is one to assess the *degree* to which Hinckley's ability to behave lawfully on March 30, 1981, was impaired? Was Hinckley "compelled" by mental disease to attempt to kill the President? Was his capacity to choose not to do so *substantially* impaired? We know that he *did not* choose to forego the assassination attempt. How can we know that he *could not* have chosen to forego the attempt?

e See page 90, above.

Assume the worst case from the government's perspective as to Hinckley's mental disease, that is, that Hinckley was indeed psychotic at the time of the offense. Does it follow that he therefore lacked the capacity to make choices about his behavior? The defense experts conceded on cross-examination that Hinckley "chose" to behave lawfully on earlier occasions when he was stalking President Carter and President-elect Reagan, despite the fact that he was being "compelled" by the same intra-psychic forces that "drove" him to act on March 30. Is it possible to determine on any basis other than his conduct itself whether he was able to act otherwise than he did on March 30?

These are hard questions. Because they are hard, and because of doubts as to whether they can be answered accurately in any situation, many law-reformers have urged that the "volitional" prong of the Model Penal Code test should be eliminated from the insanity defense. Some of the arguments in support of this reform are summarized at pages 127–31 below. As noted there, moreover, this reform was adopted by the federal government and in many states following the *Hinckley* verdict.

Consider the likely outcome if the volitional part of the Model Penal Code test had not been applicable to Hinckley's trial, that is, if the sole question had been whether Hinckley could appreciate the wrongfulness of his act. How important was the "volitional" test to Hinckley's defense? Would the verdict have been different if the jury had been instructed solely in terms of the "appreciation" part of the Model Penal Code test? Consider also whether limitation of the criteria for insanity in this manner would have made a difference in the nature of the defense testimony. If you were the judge, would you have admitted the defense testimony about the "compulsions" under which Hinckley was operating because it was relevant to whether the "appreciation" standard was met?

Some people believe that the critical question in an insanity defense is not the standard given to the jury in the instructions (the jury is unlikely in any event, the argument goes, to understand the legal subtleties involved), but the latitude that is afforded the defense experts to testify about the background and emotional history of the defendant. Notice in this connection the difference between the tactics of the government and the tactics of the defense in the *Hinckley* trial. The government tried to focus the attention of the jury on the events of March 30, emphasizing their apparent rationality in terms of a person planning to accomplish a particular objective. The defense, on the other hand, tried to divert the attention of the jury from these events, and instead to focus the jury on the development of Hinckley's condition over a long period of time prior to the offense. The government, in short, wanted to confine the jury's frame of reference to the specific events of the day of the crime; the defense wanted to expand the frame of reference to Hinckley's entire life history.

These are typical tactics in the trial of an insanity defense. Would you subscribe to the view that the important point for the defense is to get as much evidence about the defendant's background and mental condition before the jury as possible, and that the ability to do this is far more important than the precise words in the jury instructions? What was the total impact of the testimony in the *Hinckley* case? Was it the total impact of the testimony that probably led to Hinckley's acquittal, rather than close analysis by the jury of the precise wording of the instructions? If so, is this the proper basis on which an insanity defense should be judged? If not, what can and should be done to change the system?

5. Burden of Proof. Judge Parker instructed the jury to acquit Hinckley by reason of insanity unless the government proved, beyond a reasonable doubt, that he was "sane." This instruction was in accord at the time of Hinckley's trial with the law in the District of Columbia, in other federal courts, and in about half the states. Many observers believe that this instruction left the jury "no lawful choice" except to acquit Hinckley.[f]

Do you agree with this observation? Arguably, a "reasonable doubt" exists in any case where conflicting evidence reflects a reasonable difference of clinical opinion. If this is so, it may seem that all the defendant needs to do is find some experts who will testify believably for the defense. One answer to this possibility is to change the law on this point and make the defendant prove insanity in order to gain an acquittal. As developed below, pages 132–33, this reform has been adopted in many jurisdictions in the wake of the *Hinckley* case. Would it have made a difference if Hinckley had been required to prove that he was insane? If so, would the difference have been desirable?

6. Disposition. Following his acquittal, Hinckley was committed to St. Elizabeth's Hospital pursuant to the procedures outlined in the last paragraph of Judge Parker's instructions to the jury. Automatic commitment was required by a District of Columbia statute which Congress had made applicable to persons prosecuted for federal crimes in the District of Columbia and acquitted by reason of insanity.[g] Under this statute, a person committed after an insanity acquittal is entitled to request a judicial hearing 50 days after the commitment, and every six months thereafter, at which she or he bears the burden of proving eligibility for release. In order to carry this burden, the committed patient must prove, by a preponderance of the evidence, that "sanity" has been restored and that she or he will not "in the reasonable future" be a danger to self or others.

[f] See, e.g., Cohen, "It's a Mad, Mad Verdict," The New Republic, July 12, 1982, p. 13.

[g] In 1984, Congress enacted a new dispositional procedure that now applies, on a nationwide basis, to all persons acquitted of a federal crime by reason of insanity.

As of this writing, Hinckley has not been released. Issues related to his treatment and eligibility for release are considered in Part IV below.

REFORM OF THE INSANITY DEFENSE AFTER *HINCKLEY*

1. Introduction. The *Hinckley* trial crystallized public discomfort with the insanity defense and its administration, and triggered legislative activity throughout the country. Several different reforms were suggested. These included narrowing or even abolishing the defense altogether, shifting the burden of proof on insanity claims to the defendant, supplementing the "not guilty by reason of insanity" verdict with a separate verdict of "guilty but mentally ill," and restricting the scope of expert testimony. Some of these proposals were endorsed by prestigious national organizations. The American Bar Association, the American Psychiatric Association, and the National Conference of Commissioners on Uniform State Laws all recommended that the insanity defense be cut back by elimination of the "volitional" part of the inquiry. The National Commission on the Insanity Defense, an organization sponsored by the National Mental Health Association, suggested that the defendant bear the burden of proof on insanity claims. And the American Medical Association called for outright abolition of the defense.

During a three-year period following the *Hinckley* acquittal, Congress and half of the states enacted changes in the insanity defense, all designed to limit it in some respect. Congress and nine states narrowed the substantive test of insanity; Congress and seven states shifted the burden of proof to the defendant; eight states supplemented the insanity verdict with a separate verdict of guilty but mentally ill; and one state (Utah) abolished the defense altogether.[a]

2. Narrowing the Defense. Because the Model Penal Code insanity defense was employed in the *Hinckley* trial—and was then the governing criterion in a majority of states and in the federal courts—subsequent proposals to modify the defense have focused on the Model Code.

For example, Richard Bonnie argued that the "volitional" or "control" aspect of the insanity defense should be eliminated and the definition of mental disease narrowed. In The Moral Basis of the Insanity Defense, 69 A.B.A.J. 194, 196–97 (1983), he said:

> The Model Penal Code has had an extraordinary impact on criminal law. For this we should be thankful, but I believe the Code approach to criminal responsibility should be rejected. Psychiatric concepts of mental abnormality remain fluid and imprecise, and most academic commentary within the last 10

[a] For an empirical study of the impact of these reforms in five states, see Henry Steadman, Before and After *Hinckley* (1993).

years continues to question the scientific basis for assessment of volitional incapacity.

The volitional inquiry probably would be manageable if the insanity defense were permitted only in cases involving psychotic disorders. When the control test is combined with a loose or broad interpretation of the term "mental disease," however, the inevitable result is unstructured clinical speculation regarding the "causes" of criminal behavior in any case in which a defendant can be said to have a personality disorder, an impulse disorder, or any other diagnosable abnormality.

For example, it is clear enough in theory that the insanity defense is not supposed to be a ground for acquittal of persons with weak behavior controls who misbehave because of anger, jealousy, fear, or some other strong emotion. These emotions may account for a large proportion of all homicides and other assaultive crimes. Many crimes are committed by persons who are not acting "normally" and who are emotionally disturbed at the time. It is not uncommon to say that they are temporarily "out of their minds." But this is not what the law means or should mean by "insanity." Because the control test, as now construed in most states, entitles defendants to insanity instructions on the basis of these claims, I am convinced that the test involves an unacceptable risk of abuse and mistake.

It might be argued, of course, that the risk of mistake should be tolerated if the volitional prong of the defense is morally necessary. The question may be put this way: Are there clinically identifiable cases involving defendants whose behavior controls were so pathologically impaired that they ought to be acquitted although their ability to appreciate the wrongfulness of their actions was unimpaired? I do not think so. The most clinically compelling cases of volitional impairment involve the so-called impulse disorders—pyromania, kleptomania, and the like. These disorders involve severely abnormal compulsions that ought to be taken into account in sentencing, but the exculpation of pyromaniacs would be out of touch with commonly shared moral intuitions.

Bonnie concluded that the sole test of legal insanity should be whether the defendant, as a result of mental disease or mental retardation, "was unable to appreciate the wrongfulness of his conduct at the time of the offense." He further proposed that "mental disease and mental retardation" should be defined to "include only those severely abnormal mental conditions that grossly and demonstrably impair a person's perception or understanding of reality."

Modification of the insanity defense along these lines was endorsed by the American Bar Association[b] and the American Psychiatric Association.[c] In the course of an official statement on the defense issued in December, 1982, the American Psychiatric Association explained its position as follows:

> There is no perfect correlation ... between legal insanity standards and psychiatric or mental states that defendants exhibit and which psychiatrists describe. For example, while some legal scholars and practitioners believe that using the word "appreciate" (rather than "knowing" or "understanding") expands the insanity dialogue to include a broader and more comprehensive view of human behavior and thinking, this may not necessarily be so. Of much greater practical significance is whether the standard employed is interpreted by individual trial judges to permit or not permit psychiatric testimony concerning the broad range of mental functioning of possible relevance for a jury's deliberation. But this matter is not easily legislated.
>
> [This] does not mean that given the present state of psychiatric knowledge psychiatrists cannot present meaningful testimony relevant to determining a defendant's understanding or appreciation of his act. Many psychiatrists ... believe that psychiatric information relevant to determining whether a defendant understood the nature of his act, and whether he appreciated its wrongfulness, is more reliable and has a stronger scientific basis than, for example, does psychiatric information relevant to whether a defendant was able to control his behavior. The line between an irresistible impulse and an impulse not resisted is probably no sharper than that between twilight and dusk. Psychiatry is a deterministic discipline that views all human behavior as, to a good extent, "caused." The concept of volition is the subject of some disagreement among psychiatrists. Many psychiatrists therefore believe that psychiatric testimony (particularly that of a conclusory nature) about volition is more likely to produce confusion for jurors than is psychiatric testimony relevant to a defendant's appreciation or understanding.
>
> Another major consideration in articulating standards for the insanity defense is the definition of mental disease or defect.... Allowing insanity acquittals in cases involving persons who manifest primarily "personality disorders" such as antisocial personality disorder (sociopathy) does not accord with modern psychiatric knowledge or psychiatric beliefs concerning

[b] American Bar Association Policy on the Insanity Defense, Approved by the ABA House of Delegates, February 9, 1983.

[c] American Psychiatric Association Statement on the Insanity Defense (December, 1982).

the extent to which such persons do have control over their behavior. Persons with antisocial personality disorders should, at least for heuristic reasons, be held accountable for their behavior. The American Psychiatric Association, therefore, suggests that any revision of the insanity defense standards should indicate that mental disorders potentially leading to exculpation must be serious. Such disorders should usually be of the severity (if not always of the quality) of conditions that psychiatrists diagnose as psychoses.

The standard recently proposed by Bonnie is one which the American Psychiatric Association believes does permit relevant psychiatric testimony to be brought to bear on the great majority of cases where criminal responsibility is at issue. . . .

In practice there is considerable overlap between a psychotic person's defective understanding or appreciation and his ability to control his behavior. Most psychotic persons who fail a volitional test for insanity will also fail a cognitive-type test when such a test is applied to their behavior, thus rendering the volitional test superfluous in judging them.

The revision adopted by the Congress to govern the insanity defense in prosecutions for federal crimes followed this approach. Until 1984, no federal statute addressed the insanity defense. Although the Supreme Court had ruled in 1895 that the government was required to disprove insanity when that defense was raised, the Court had never ruled on the appropriate content of the insanity defense in federal courts. That left the issue to regional resolution by the several United States Circuit Courts of Appeal. As noted above, by the time of the *Hinckley* trial each of the federal circuits had adopted tests based on the Model Penal Code that included both the cognitive and the volitional prongs of the Model Code defense. The 1984 legislation changed this approach by requiring a "severe" mental disease and eliminating the volitional part of the defense.[d] The new federal statute, codified at 18 U.S.C. § 20, provides:

It is an affirmative defense to a prosecution under any federal statute that, at the time of the commission of the acts constituting the offense, the defendant as a result of a severe mental disease or defect, was unable to appreciate the nature and quality or the wrongfulness of his acts. Mental disease or defect does not otherwise constitute a defense.

Is this result sound? Should the "volitional" or "control" aspect of the insanity defense be abolished? Should the definition of mental disease be narrowed? Would these changes prevent abuses of the insanity defense? Or would they result in the conviction of persons who are, in

[d] In United States v. Lyons, 731 F.2d 243, 15 Fed. R. Evid. Serv. 859, (5th Cir. 1984) (en banc), the court anticipated the eventual congressional action by abandoning the volitional prong of the Model Penal Code test.

some sense, undeserving of criminal punishment? What would be their practical impact in the courtroom in terms of limiting the range of expert testimony or reducing the indeterminacy of the insanity defense?

3. The Verdict of "Guilty But Mentally Ill." About one-fourth of the states have established a separate verdict of "guilty but mentally ill" (hereafter GBMI). The GBMI concept, as adopted in these states, should be distinguished from two other concepts to which this or similar terminology may refer.

First, the GBMI verdict is available as an alternative to, rather than instead of, the verdict of "not guilty by reason of insanity." The jury, in other words, is given four verdict options: guilty, guilty but mentally ill, not guilty, or not guilty by reason of insanity. This procedure is thus completely different from abolition of the insanity defense and establishing in its stead a special procedure for the commitment of guilty but mentally ill defendants, as has been done in Montana, Idaho, and Utah.[e]

Second, the consequence of a GBMI verdict is conviction and a criminal sentence. The GBMI procedure is, therefore, also different from renaming the verdict following an insanity acquittal (changing it from "not guilty by reason of insanity" to "guilty but insane") without altering its consequences in any other respect. This has been done in Maryland.[f]

The GBMI verdict is based on different conclusions by the jury in different states. Under most of the statutes, the jury is asked to determine whether the defendant was "mentally ill" (though not legally insane) at the time of the offense. The definition of "mental illness" used for this purpose is typically drawn from the state's civil commitment statute and is usually much broader than the "mental disease" required for the insanity defense. In Michigan, for example, mental illness for purposes of the GBMI verdict is defined as "a substantial disorder of thought or mood which significantly impairs judgment, behavior, capacity to recognize reality, or ability to cope with the ordinary demands of life." Obviously, a great many persons convicted of violent crime might be found "mentally ill" under this standard even though they would not be entitled to acquittal by reason of insanity.

In a few states, however, the required finding is linked to grounds which elsewhere would establish an insanity defense. In Delaware, for example, the exclusive basis for an insanity defense is "lack of substantial capacity to appreciate wrongfulness," whereas a GBMI verdict can be based on volitional impairment—that is, that the defendant suffered from a "psychiatric disorder" which "left [him] with insufficient willpower to choose whether he would do the act or refrain from doing it." In Alaska, an insanity defense is available only if the defendant was

[e] See page 135, below.

[f] See Pouncey v. State, 297 Md. 264, 465 A.2d 475 (1983).

"unable ... to appreciate the nature and quality of his conduct." A verdict of "guilty but mentally ill" is permitted, on the other hand, if this standard is not met but the more generous Model Penal Code insanity test is satisfied.

Procedures under GBMI legislation vary significantly from state to state. Typically, the statutes provide that, following a verdict of guilty but mentally ill, the trial judge will impose an ordinary criminal sentence. The defendant is then evaluated by correctional or mental health authorities to determine her or his suitability for psychiatric treatment. If the evaluators conclude that such treatment is warranted, the person is hospitalized for that purpose. Upon discharge, the individual is returned to prison to serve the remainder of the criminal sentence. In practice, whether the prisoner will be placed in a mental health facility or will remain confined in an ordinary correctional institution is typically a discretionary determination made by the correctional or mental health authorities without intervention by the trial judge.

The debate about GBMI legislation focuses in part on the dispositional consequences. The GBMI verdict is designed to facilitate psychiatric treatment of mentally disordered offenders. Some critics charge, however, that the procedure is misleading, because it does not, in fact, assure treatment. Additionally, critics claim that a separate verdict of GBMI is not needed to facilitate treatment of disordered offenders. Without regard to a GBMI verdict, all states either operate psychiatric hospitals within the correctional system or have well-established procedures for transferring prisoners to secure mental health facilities. Finally, the critics say, a jury verdict based on evidence of past mental condition is an awkward device for triggering a disposition inquiry based on the defendant's present mental condition.

As these observations suggest, the actual impact of the GBMI procedure on the sentencing and correctional process may be slight. Perhaps of greater importance is the effect of the GBMI procedure on the adjudication of guilt or innocence. It may, therefore, be appropriate to ask: What is the intended effect of the GBMI verdict? Is it designed, perhaps, to subvert the insanity defense? Is it plausible to believe that there might be fewer acquittals by reason of insanity if the GBMI verdict were an available option? If so, is that a legitimate reason to endorse the GBMI procedure?

4. Burden of Proof. One much-debated feature of the insanity defense after the *Hinckley* verdict has been on whom the burden of proof should be placed. Allocation of the burden of proof may play an important role in close cases. It determines which side—prosecution or defense—will lose if the jury finds itself unable to determine (with whatever degree of certainty the law may specify) whether the defendant was or was not legally insane.

At the time of Hinckley's trial, a bare majority of states required the prosecution to disprove a defendant's insanity claim beyond a reasonable doubt. In the aftermath of the *Hinckley* case, that position has been reconsidered. Today, in two-thirds of the states recognizing the defense, the defendant bears the burden of persuading the jury that she or he was in fact insane, usually by a preponderance of the evidence. Under the new federal statute, the defendant bears a more demanding burden. As that statute states: "The defendant has the burden of proving the defense of insanity by clear and convincing evidence."[g]

5. The "Battle of the Experts." Many proposals to narrow the availability of the insanity defense reflect an undercurrent of skepticism about the reliability of psychiatric testimony. Such doubts can only have been reinforced by the contradictory opinions uttered by the experts in the *Hinckley* trial. Syndicated columnist George F. Will expressed these widely shared views with characteristic pungency:[h]

> The [*Hinckley*] trial allowed—indeed, required—a jury to pick between numerous flatly incompatible theories spun by credentialed "experts," theories purporting to divine Hinckley's mental state on one day 15 months [before the trial]. Some alarmed lawyers propose restricting psychiatric testimony to statements of fact—what psychiatrists see or hear. But psychiatrists are often hired to put an acre of embroidery around a pinhead of "fact." So they bandy diagnostic categories that are as evanescent as snowflakes, swapping bald assertions with the serenity of philistines operating far from serious intellectual criteria.
>
> ... Psychiatry as practiced by some of today's itinerant experts-for-hire is this century's alchemy. No, that is unfair to alchemists, who were confused but honest. Some of today's rent-a-psychiatry is charlatanism laced with cynicism.

In its official statement on the insanity defense issued in the wake of the *Hinckley* trial,[i] the American Psychiatric Association acknowledged the widespread public criticism of "the nature and quality of psychiatric testimony in insanity trials." While not commenting specifically on the *Hinckley* case, the APA pointed out that the so-called "battle of the experts" is "to a certain extent foreordained by the structure of the adversary system," and is in any event not limited to psychiatry:

> Experts often disagree in many types of criminal and civil trials. For example, other medical experts may disagree on the

[g] The constitutionality of requiring the defendant to prove insanity (rather than requiring the government to disprove that claim) has apparently been settled. See Leland v. Oregon, 343 U.S. 790, 72 S.Ct. 1002 (1952); Rivera v. Delaware, 429 U.S. 877, 97 S.Ct. 226 (1976).

[h] Washington Post, June 23, 1982, page A27, col. 1.

[i] American Psychiatric Association, Statement on the Insanity Defense, December, 1982.

interpretation of x-rays, engineers on structural issues, and economists on market concentration issues. American jurisprudence requires each side (defense and prosecutor) to make the best case it can in the search for the just outcome.

The APA also disputed the degree of disagreement among psychiatrists about scientific or clinical issues. "In fact," the APA asserted, "the prosecution and defense psychiatrists [often] agree about the nature and even the extent of mental disorder exhibited by the defendant at the time of the act." Disagreements are most likely to arise in connection with the so-called "ultimate issues"—e.g., whether the defendant did or did not lack substantial capacity to conform his or her behavior to the requirements of law. On this dimension of the controversy—the propriety of expert opinion testimony on ultimate issues—the APA joined hands with the critics of expert testimony:

> The American Psychiatric Association is not opposed to legislatures restricting psychiatric testimony about the . . . ultimate legal issues concerning the insanity defense. We adopt this position because it is clear that psychiatrists are experts in medicine, not the law. As such, the psychiatrist's first obligation and expertise in the courtroom is to "do psychiatry," i.e., to present medical information and opinion about the defendant's mental state and motivation and to explain in detail the reason for his medical-psychiatric conclusions. When, however, "ultimate issue" questions are formulated by the law and put to the expert witness who must then say "yea" or "nay," then the expert witness is required to make a leap in logic. He no longer addresses himself to medical concepts but instead must infer or intuit what is in fact unspeakable, namely, the *probable relationship* between medical concepts and legal or moral constructs such as free will. These impermissible leaps in logic made by expert witnesses confuse the jury. Juries thus find themselves listening to conclusory and seemingly contradictory psychiatric testimony that defendants are either "sane" or "insane" or that they do or do not meet the relevant legal test for insanity. . . .

> Psychiatrists, of course, must be permitted to testify fully about the defendant's psychiatric diagnosis, mental state and motivation (in clinical and commonsense terms) at the time of the alleged act so as to permit the jury or judge to reach the ultimate conclusion about which they, and only they, are expert. Determining whether a criminal defendant was legally insane is a matter for legal factfinders, not for experts.

As it happens, the experts who testified in the *Hinckley* case not only reached different conclusions on the so-called "ultimate" issues, but also offered widely divergent diagnoses of Hinckley's condition. However, the case nonetheless presents an opportunity to assess the significance of proposals to bar ultimate-issue testimony. Consider, for example, the language included on this point in the statute enacted by the Congress in 1984:

> No expert witness testifying with respect to the mental state or condition of a defendant in a criminal case may state an opinion or inference as to whether the defendant did or did not have the mental state or condition constituting an element of the crime charged or of a defense thereto. Such ultimate issues are matters for the trier of fact alone.

Where would the line between permissible and impermissible testimony be drawn under this statute? Obviously, the experts would not have been permitted to say whether or not Hinckley "lacked substantial capacity" to appreciate the wrongfulness of his conduct or to conform his conduct to the requirements of law. But would they have been permitted to express opinions on whether or not he was "driven" by a "compulsion" to shoot President Reagan? On whether he "knew" it was wrong to shoot the President? On whether his ability to "appreciate the wrongfulness" of his acts was "impaired" or "diminished?" Would the testimony in the *Hinckley* case have been significantly different if ultimate-issue testimony had been barred? Would the closing arguments have been different? Would the restriction now imposed by the federal statute likely have made any difference?[j]

6. Abolition of the Insanity Defense. Three states (Montana, Idaho, and Utah) have abolished insanity as a separate defense. These states do, however, admit evidence of mental disorder for the narrow purpose of proving that the defendant did not have any special knowledge or intent required for conviction of the offense charged. If this position had been taken in the *Hinckley* case, evidence of Hinckley's mental condition would have been admissible, for example, only if it could show that Hinckley did not intend to kill the President. If, as seems inescapable on the testimony offered, the evidence was not admitted or, if admitted, the jury found that Hinckley intended to kill the President, the fact that he may not have appreciated the significance of murder or that he may not have been able to control his impulse to commit it would not have mattered. Insanity would not have been recognized as a separate defense.

This position has been endorsed by the American Medical Association.[k] The leading academic proponent of this view is Professor Norval Morris. In Madness and the Criminal Law 61–64 (1982), Professor Morris summarized his position as follows:[*]

[j] For discussion of these puzzles, see Christopher Slobogin, The Ultimate Issue Issue, 7 Behav. Sci. & the Law 259 (1989).

[k] Insanity Defense in Criminal Trials and Limitations of Psychiatric Testimony, Report of Board of Trustees, Committee on Medicolegal Problems, American Medical Association, 251 J.A.M.A. 2967 (1984).

[*] Reprinted from Madness and the Criminal Law by N. Morris with permission of the University of Chicago Press. © 1982 The University of Chicago Press.

[The insanity defense rests on] the sense that it is unjust and unfair to stigmatize the mentally ill as criminals and to punish them for their crimes. The criminal law exists to deter and to punish those who would or who do choose to do wrong. If they cannot exercise choice, they cannot be deterred and it is a moral outrage to punish them. The argument sounds powerful but its premise is weak.

Choice is neither present nor absent in the typical case where the insanity defense is currently pleaded; what is at issue is the degree of freedom of choice on a continuum from the hypothetically entirely rational to the hypothetically pathologically determined—in states of consciousness neither polar condition exists.

The moral issue sinks into the sands of reality. Certainly it is true that in a situation of total absence of choice it is outrageous to inflict punishment; but the frequency of such situations to the problems of criminal responsibility becomes an issue of fact in which tradition and clinical knowledge and practice are in conflict. The traditions of being possessed of evil spirits, of being bewitched, confront the practices of a mental health system which increasingly fashions therapeutic practices to hold patients responsible for their conduct. . . .

[M]ajor contributors to jurisprudence and criminal law theory insist that it is necessary to maintain the denial of responsibility on grounds of mental illness to preserve the moral infrastructure of the criminal law. For many years I have struggled with this opinion by those whose work I deeply respect, yet I remain unpersuaded. Indeed, they really don't try to persuade, but rather affirm and reaffirm with vehemence and almost mystical sincerity the necessity of retaining the special defense of insanity as a moral prop to the entire criminal law.

And indeed I think that much of the discussion of the defense of insanity is the discussion of a myth rather than of a reality. It is no minor debating point that in fact we lack a defense of insanity as an operating tool of the criminal law other than in relation to a very few particularly heinous and heavily punished offenses. There is not an operating defense of insanity in relation to burglary or theft, or the broad sweep of [ordinary] crimes generally; the plea of not guilty on the ground of insanity is rarely to be heard in city courts of first instance which handle the grist of the mill of the criminal law—though a great deal of pathology is to be seen in the parade of accused and convicted persons before these courts. As a practical matter we reserve this defense for a few sensational cases where it may be in the interest of the accused either to escape the possibility of capital punishment (though in cases where serious mental illness is present, the risk of execution is slight) or where the likely punishment is of a sufficient severity to make the indeterminate commitment of the accused a preferable alternative to a criminal conviction. Operationally the defense of insanity is a tribute, it seems to me, to our hypocrisy rather than to our morality.

[T]he special defense of insanity may properly be indicted as producing a morally unsatisfactory classification on the continuum between guilt and innocence. It applies in practice to only a few mentally ill criminals, thus omitting many others with guilt-reducing relationships between their mental illness and their crime; it excludes other powerful pressures on human behavior, thus giving excessive weight to the psychological over the social. It is a false classification in the sense that if a team of the world's most sensitive and trained psychiatrists and moralists were to select from all those found guilty of felonies and those found not guilty by reason of insanity any given number who should not be stigmatized as criminals, very few of those found not guilty by reason of insanity would be selected. How to offer proof of this? The only proof, I regret, is to be found by personal contact with a flow of felony cases through the courts and into the prisons. No one of serious perception will fail to recognize both the extent of mental illness and retardation among the prison population and the overwhelming weight of adverse social circumstances on criminal behavior. This is, of course, not an argument that social adversities should lead to acquittals; they should be taken into account in sentencing. And the same is true of the guilt and sentencing of those pressed by psychological adversities.

The issue of whether to abolish the insanity defense requires a return to the premise of the defense with which these materials began, as developed on pages 3–5 above. As there noted, and as Professor Morris elaborates, proponents of the insanity defense argue that some independent measure of legal insanity is necessary to take account of the moral foundations of the criminal law and the morally significant effects of mental illness. Professor Morris contends, to the contrary, that mentally disordered offenders who had the knowledge or intent required by the definition of the offense *are* morally blameworthy and are, therefore, proper subjects for criminal punishment. Who is right? Is the insanity defense essential to the moral integrity of the criminal law, as its proponents contend? Or do you agree with Professor Morris' view that it represents a "morally false" classification? If John Hinckley satisfied the legal criteria for the insanity defense, should he nonetheless have been held responsible for his behavior on March 30, 1981?

———

*

PART IV

THE AFTERMATH

HOSPITALIZATION AND TREATMENT OF JOHN W. HINCKLEY, JR.: THE FIRST FIFTEEN YEARS

1. Automatic Commitment (1982). Following his insanity acquittal in June 1982, John Hinckley was committed to St. Elizabeth's Hospital in the District of Columbia. Automatic commitment was required by the statute applicable at the time.[a]

Hinckley was entitled to request a judicial release hearing after 50 days, and every six months thereafter. Under the statutory scheme, the insanity verdict triggers a legal presumption that an insanity acquittee is mentally ill and dangerous at the time of commitment and remains so thereafter until such time as the acquitted person can prove otherwise.[b] In order to establish his eligibility for release, Hinckley bears the burden of proving, by a preponderance of the evidence, that his "sanity" has been restored and that he will not "in the reasonable future" be a danger to himself or others.

The statute requires judicial approval not only for discharge from the hospital (whether conditionally or unconditionally) but also for any temporary release that removes the patient from the custody of the hospital staff. As a practical matter, the prospect that a court will approve an acquittee's release request—whether temporary or permanent, conditional or unconditional—will be strongly influenced by the recommendation of the hospital authorities. Although courts usually ratify release requests supported by the hospital, they rarely approve requests opposed by the hospital.

Hinckley did not request a release hearing after the expiration of the initial 50–day period. His first release hearing was not held until June, 1997, some 15 years after he was committed. Between 1982 and 1997, however, he did file several legal complaints about the restrictiveness of his confinement, as well as several requests for temporary release. The early litigation is summarized below, followed by the District Court's ruling on his 1997 request for conditional release.

[a] In 1984, Congress enacted a new dispositional procedure. It applies, on a nationwide basis, to all persons acquitted of a federal crime by reason of insanity after the effective date of the statute. It does not apply to insanity acquittals before that date, and for that reason does not apply to Hinckley.

[b] In Jones v. United States, 463 U.S. 354, 103 S.Ct. 3043 (1983), the Supreme Court held that the District of Columbia's commitment procedure was constitutional.

2. Initial Complaints (1984–1986). Like most insanity acquittees at St. Elizabeth's Hospital, Hinckley was initially hospitalized in a
maximum security facility (the John Howard Pavilion) separated from
the units where ordinary "civil" patients reside. In August 1984, he
petitioned the District Court to loosen the "severe restrictions" of his
confinement. Although he did not request transfer to a civil unit, he did
challenge hospital practices restricting his access to a telephone, prohib-
iting media interviews, and denying him limited "grounds privileges."
He asked for an opportunity to leave the building and to walk on the
hospital grounds for an hour a day accompanied by a staff member. At a
hearing on October 4, 1984, Hinckley testified as follows:

> When I arrived at St. Elizabeth's Hospital on June 22,
> 1982, I did have mental problems. I was out of control two years
> ago and the restrictions placed upon me at that time were
> appropriate. Looking back now, I can see that I definitely
> needed mail and telephone and interview restrictions because
> my illness led me to do and write and say some very stupid and
> very sick things. At the time, I didn't appreciate these restric-
> tions on me, but now I can see that they were necessary and
> protected me from myself. I no longer need protection from
> myself. These severe restrictions have become unfair and unnec-
> essary. . . .

> I am perhaps the only patient in John Howard Pavilion that
> cannot make local phone calls without the staff dialing my
> number and checking on the other party. This policy of monitor-
> ing my phone calls has become unfair and totally unneces-
> sary. . . .

> On the issue of giving interview to media representatives
> . . ., I would like to be able to give an occasional interview to
> media representatives whom I can trust, but the hospital says
> no to any patient giving interviews. . . . It is quite obvious that
> the interview restriction at St. Elizabeth's was written up with
> John Hinckley in mind. I am, of course, the most well-known
> patient at the hospital and just about the only patient that the
> media cares about and wants to interview. . . .

> Your Honor, I can see now that I did need that interview
> restriction in the summer of '82 because my judgment was poor
> and my delusions about Jodie Foster were so strong that I was
> capable of saying some very outrageous things. But now my
> doctors and I believe that my judgment is much better and my
> obsession with Jodie Foster has been over for 19 months. . . .

> I think I am ready, too, for limited ground privileges. . . . I
> deserve [such] privileges now because my doctors say I am
> clinically ready for them. It should not take more than a week
> or two to work out the security precautions. I would be willing

to wear a bulletproof vest and walk with an armed guard if that is what the hospital or court wants.

All I want is the chance to have my therapy in the sunshine for a change away from the walls and fences and bars and every other depressing thing. The atmosphere at John Howard Pavilion can be suffocating at times and it would be the best therapy in the world for me to breathe fresh air away from that building an hour a day or an hour a week if the court feels that is more appropriate.

Your Honor, it has been two and one-half years since the assassination attempt and a lot has happened during that time. I spent 13 months in a very depressed state of mind waiting for trial.

On June 21, 1982, I was found not guilty by reason of insanity and the next day I was taken to St. Elizabeth's Hospital to begin my recovery. My first six months at the hospital were bleak because I was still obsessed, depressed, and desperate.

At the height of my despair on February 13, 1983, I attempted suicide and, thank God, I failed. Nothing has been the same since that suicide attempt.

I overcame the obsession with Jodie Foster through intense therapy, medication, and a lot of love from the people around me. For the first time in years, I was glad to be alive and each day became an exciting challenge and adventure.

I now cherish my life and believe that everyone's life is sacred and precious. I will never again harm another human being.

Your Honor, I am ready for some responsibility. I am asking you to lift the interview and telephone restrictions and let me walk the grounds of the hospital accompanied by staff.

Please give me the opportunity to prove to you and the hospital and the entire world that I am getting well.

Thank you.

The U.S. Attorney's office opposed all of Hinckley's requests, which had been previously rejected by his "treatment team" and by the hospital's "Forensic Review Board." The government argued that each of the requests pertained "to decisions regarding his treatment [that] are uniquely within the clinical and administrative discretion of the hospital staff" and that these decisions should be reviewed by the court only to determine whether the hospital had abused its discretion. To demonstrate that the hospital's decisions were reasonable, the government submitted affidavits by Hinckley's psychiatrist and by other hospital officials. These affidavits explained that the staff had recently removed restrictions on Hinckley's correspondence, based in part on the improvement in his condition and in part on his agreement to show his psychiatrists any letters to the media before sending them. The staff concluded, however, that Hinckley should be denied unrestricted use of the telephone until he had "demonstrated an ability to handle in a responsible manner the increased freedom of unscreened correspondence." The staff also felt that personal interviews with the media "would adversely affect [Hinckley's] clinical progress and his working though underlying psychodynamic issues." Finally, the staff concluded that "any type of grounds privileges would be inappropriate at this time, both for clinical and security reasons."

At the hearing before federal District Judge Barrington Parker, who had presided over Hinckley's trial, Hinckley's psychiatrist testified that even though Hinckley's condition had improved, she thought that all of the restrictions continued to be appropriate. Judge Parker denied all of Hinckley's requests, concluding that "there is complete justification and sound reasoning for the restrictions currently imposed."

In early 1986, Hinckley filed *pro se* requests (i.e., on his own, without legal representation) asking to be moved to a less restrictive ward at St. Elizabeth's than the maximum-security John Howard Pavilion and to be allowed to leave St. Elizabeth's on unsupervised trips to downtown Washington once a month. At the time, he had only recently been allowed to walk the grounds in the company of hospital personnel on a regular basis. The hospital opposed Hinckley's requests because, although he was no longer psychotic or depressive, he still had "a serious narcissistic personality disorder" and "lacked insight and judgment about his illness." Thus, the hospital stated in its affidavit, "it is not possible to state that Mr. Hinckley would not present a danger to the community." After a hearing, in March 1986, Judge Parker denied the requests.

Hinckley's continuing interest in fame was evident in his constant contact with the media during this period. A March 1985 *Washington Post* article, which reported that *New York Post* writer George Carpozi had been in touch with Hinckley about a book deal, described Hinckley as a "compulsive writer of letters to reporters." A *Washington Post* interview with his parents in May of the same year revealed that he had made an "unauthorized" phone call to the *Post* to say that when he saw James Brady on the ground immediately after shooting him, "it was like it was just a mannequin. I had no emotion about it. I really feel sorry for him now." The same article reported that Hinckley wrote to *Newsweek* comparing himself to Andrei Sakharov and offering himself to the Soviets in exchange for the dissident physicist. And shortly after Judge Parker's decision in March 1986, Hinckley wrote *The New Republic* to complain about the magazine's use of the term "funny farm" to describe St. Elizabeth's.

On December 28, 1986, the hospital's review board felt Hinckley had progressed enough to allow a supervised 12–hour visit with his family for the holidays. Although court approval was not sought for this supervised outing (because it did not involve a release from hospital custody), the hospital notified both the court and the Secret Service of the planned outing. U.S. Attorney Joseph diGenova acknowledged that "Hinckley was released under a statute that does not require permission from the court," but went on to say that "if there had been a request for the court's permission, we would have opposed his release, because we do not believe that anyone who tries to nullify a national election with a bullet deserves the privilege of moving freely in a civilized society."

3. Aborted Request for Unsupervised Release (1987). In April 1987, believing that Hinckley's progress had continued, the hospital requested the court's approval for a short Easter visit with his family. Unlike the 1986 Christmas visit with his family, this request required court approval because Hinckley would not have been supervised by hospital staff. In support of its request, the hospital indicated that Hinckley was no longer required to take antipsychotic medication, was allowed to "travel unaccompanied to and from his work assignment," and had developed an apparently healthy romantic relationship with former fellow inmate Leslie deVeau. Members of his treatment team went so far as to suggest that he "might soon be a candidate" for conditional discharge from the hospital. The government opposed the request and additionally asked to be notified in advance of any future off-grounds visit, whether supervised or unsupervised.

In preparation for the upcoming release hearing, prosecutors produced a 1982 letter from Hinckley to a friend, Penny Bailey, in which he asked her to mail him a pistol so he could escape; or go to New Haven to kill Foster, who was then a student at Yale University; or hijack an airplane and demand that Hinckley be released and Foster be brought to him. At the hearing itself, Hinckley's consulting psychiatrist, Dr. Glenn Miller, alluded to Hinckley's correspondence with Lynette "Squeaky" Fromme (requesting Charles Manson's address) and Ted Bundy (expressing his sympathy about being on death row). This correspondence was previously unknown to the government or to the court. These surprising disclosures prompted Judge Parker to order that "any and all writings, documents, notes, letters, post cards, correspondence and poems of any description" be turned over to the court and that other materials in Hinckley's possession be inventoried and the list provided to the court. According to Bundy, Hinckley had initiated the correspondence with him in May of 1986, and prosecutors felt the replies from Bundy found in Hinckley's possession indicated similarity between his fascination with the movie *Taxi Driver* and his interest in Bundy.

Despite Dr. Miller's confident report that Hinckley had not been obsessed with Jodie Foster "for at least three years" and that Hinckley posed no danger to her, the court-ordered search of Hinckley's room also turned up 57 photos of the actress. In the face of this new and embarrassing evidence, the hospital withdrew its request for release in order "to assess the clinical significance of writings and other materials heretofore unexamined by the hospital staff." It also agreed in a stipulated order to notify the court and the government of any proposed (supervised) visits off hospital grounds, as requested by the government.

    4. Tight Control Continues (1988–1997). In July 1988, the hospital notified the District Court and the government that it planned to take Hinckley on a supervised trip into the city, possibly with other patients. The government opposed this trip and asked the court to hold a hearing. The day before the hearing, the government turned over to the court evidence—obtained during a Secret Service investigation of Hinckley—that he had attempted to obtain a nude sketch of Jodie Foster. In light of this disclosure, the hospital announced at the hearing that it would not pursue the planned outing, saying that it had "determined that further clinical assessment by Mr. Hinckley's treatment staff is necessary."

    In the spring of 1989, Hinckley requested that Judge June Green authorize a change of counsel. Judge Green had inherited the Hinckley case after Judge Barrington Parker's death in 1988. At a hearing on his request in April 1989, hospital psychiatrist Dr. Raymond Patterson testified that Hinckley was back in the maximum security ward after "he had difficulty handling privileges." He noted the hospital's concern that if Hinckley were permitted to choose his own attorney, he might be exploited because of the notoriety of the case. In particular, Hinckley had mentioned Mark Lane, who had written about the assassinations of John F. Kennedy and Martin Luther King, Jr., and had written a number of books on people he had represented. Hinckley testified that he wanted to hire Lane because "he has represented people who are famous to the general public." Judge Green refused to place any restrictions on Hinckley's ability to retain an attorney of his own choice, but since Lane, a New York lawyer, was not on the D.C. list of approved court-appointed attorneys, the judge also denied Hinckley's request to appoint him and instead appointed a D.C. attorney. United States v. Hinckley, 721 F.Supp. 323 (D.D.C.1989).

    As it turned out, Lane subsequently represented Hinckley in a petition for access to the media in the fall of 1989 which was also opposed by the hospital. Hinckley testified on his own behalf that he was no longer on antipsychotic medication and had not been obsessed with Jodie Foster for five or six years, and he presented Dr. Glenn Miller's 1987 report in support of his testimony. On behalf of the hospital, Dr. Patterson testified that Hinckley continued to suffer predominantly from narcissistic personality disorder and continued to engage in manipulative behavior in order to obscure his continuing symptoms. Dr. Patterson said that access to media interviews would be counter-therapeutic. Judge Green agreed. She noted that Dr. Miller's judgment in 1987 stating that

Hinckley was no longer obsessed with Foster had been contradicted by the large collection of photos of the actress found in Hinckley's room. Also, the court referred to letters by Hinckley describing "his plans for his 'family,' 'cult movement,' or 'nation within a nation' " and setting forth "ideas and fascinations quite different from those expressed by the patient described in hospital records and Dr. Miller's report." For instance, Hinckley described himself in the letters as a successor to Hitler and "attempted as recently as June 1988 to convey word to Manson that "he's one cool dude" [and] a "prophet." The court concluded:

> Dr. Patterson's explanation of how Mr. Hinckley's letters matched the diagnosis was reasonable and convincing. Since the very moment of his arrest for the shooting, Mr. Hinckley has been obsessed with the media's coverage of his thoughts and deeds, his first inquiries at the police station having been "where is the media? Where is the press?" The initial diagnosis of narcissism and grandiosity has been borne out by his letters and pattern of concealment, despite intermittent assessments of his outwardly improved behavior. Though Mr. Hinckley's condition may have improved or abated over the years, substantial evidence supports Dr. Patterson's view that the instant motion is further proof that the patient's grandiose delusions and media fixation continue at this time. His view that the approval of Mr. Hinckley's request would be harmful to the defendant's therapy is a reasonable decision.

Since the decision of the hospital staff was reasonable, and since Hinckley was not forbidden from contacting media or responding to questions by mail, Judge Green upheld the constitutionality of the hospital's restrictions on media interviews. United States v. Hinckley, 725 F.Supp. 616 (D.D.C.1989).

In September 1992, Hinckley filed a request that he be allowed 12–hour unsupervised visits with his family on federal holidays. The hospital opposed this motion, saying he was still dangerous to himself and others. Hinckley's lawyer then withdrew the request before the scheduled hearing, explaining that he wanted to give the hospital time to develop a report of Hinckley's progress. A virtual repeat of the same request occurred in late 1996. Members of Hinckley's treatment team had indicated they would support unsupervised 12–hour visits, and Hinckley's attorney insisted that Hinckley was now "essentially well." However, court-appointed experts Raymond Patterson and David Shapiro (a psychologist) would have testified that they, like the hospital review board, opposed the release, so once again Hinckley's request was withdrawn before the scheduled hearing.

In 1997, Hinckley filed a motion for unsupervised release into his parents' custody for a 12–hour period once a month, still over the objections of the hospital. He also asked the court to vacate its 10-year-old order requiring the hospital to give advance notice of any supervised excursions away from the hospital. The court held a release hearing and issued the following opinion.

UNITED STATES v. JOHN W. HINCKLEY, JR.
United States District Court, District of Columbia.
967 F.Supp. 557 (1997).

JUNE L. GREEN, DISTRICT JUDGE.

... In 1981, in a failed assassination attempt, petitioner [John W. Hinckley, Jr.] shot and wounded four individuals including then-President of the United States, Ronald Reagan. At his criminal trial, petitioner presented evidence that he was suffering from a mental disease and that his criminal actions were the result of such disease. Petitioner was acquitted of the charges brought against him by reason of insanity and, following his trial, committed to St. Elizabeths Hospital ("the hospital") where he has remained since June 21, 1982.

In the nearly 16 years since his commitment began, petitioner has at various times sought some form of release from the court. Each time, petitioner's request was either denied or withdrawn. Moreover, requests by the hospital in 1987 and 1988 that Mr. Hinckley be released into the community under the supervision of hospital staff were also withdrawn.

In the motion at issue here, petitioner asks the court to release him into the community in the care of his parents, but otherwise unsupervised, for 12 hours each month. Petitioner also asks that a stipulation entered in 1987 requiring that the hospital give two-weeks notice to the court and to the United States Attorney's Office prior to any supervised excursions off the grounds of the hospital be vacated....

The petitioner presented five witnesses including four experts: two psychologists, Drs. Kirk S. Heilbrun and R. Mark Binderman; and two psychiatrists, Drs. William T. Carpenter and John J. Kelley. The petitioner's father, John Hinckley, Sr., also testified. The government, for its part, offered the testimony of a fact witness, Cmdr. Jeanette Wick, as well as its own expert psychiatrist, Dr. Raymond F. Patterson.

[T]he court is required to make findings of fact and conclusions of law with regard to whether the proposed release will benefit the patient and be safe for the public. In order for the petitioner to be successful, the court must, after weighing all of the evidence, find (by a preponderance of the evidence) that the petitioner "will not, in the reasonable future, endanger himself or others." [I]t is not "sufficient for the District Court merely to find that the patient 'is no longer likely to injure himself or other persons because of mental illness.'" The court must make an "affirmative finding that it is at least more probable than not that [petitioner] will not be violently dangerous in the future."

In receiving and weighing the evidence, the court is not bound to accept the opinion of any expert witness but is free to consider other evidence, including "the patient's hospital file, the court files and records in the case, and whatever illumination is provided by counsel."

In examining the evidence here, the court notes that the request for conditional release has not come from the hospital, but from the petitioner and that the hospital has, in fact, denied a similar request made by the petitioner. Such a posture makes an exacting review of the evidence that much more important.

Petitioner's experts were in substantial agreement concerning Mr. Hinckley's current diagnosis: that is, that petitioner suffers from psychotic disorder not otherwise specified, in remission; major depression, in remission; and, narcissistic personality disorder.[2] The opinions of the petitioner's experts essentially are that petitioner would present a very low risk of danger to himself or others should his request for conditional release be granted. These opinions were based upon the results of psychological testing, interviews with hospital staff, and review of medical records. These experts also agreed, for the most part, that petitioner's prior active mental illness was such that any symptomatic recurrence would likely progress over a period of time longer than the 12 hours involved in the requested monthly excursions. This is significant, they reasoned, because any symptoms would, therefore, be detectable in advance of an unescorted visit.

Following the close of the petitioner's case, the government offered the testimony of Cmdr. Jeanette Wick, chief pharmacist at the hospital. Cmdr. Wick testified regarding her relationship with the petitioner. She stated that she first became personally acquainted with the petitioner when she offered to lend him a book in late February or early March of 1995. Cmdr. Wick stated that Mr. Hinckley began to visit her office fairly frequently and that these visits were unannounced. During these visits, Cmdr. Wick stated that petitioner would talk about books that he was reading or wanted to read. Cmdr. Wick also testified that on these occasions, petitioner asked her advice on whether she thought he should be interviewed by Barbara Walters and gave her audio tapes of music he had recorded, including one "love song" containing the pet name of her daughter. Even more disturbing to Cmdr. Wick was her discovery that the petitioner had been gathering information about her after-hours personal schedule with her daughter.

Cmdr. Wick stated that their relationship progressed in this way (about three weeks) until she was taken aside by her staff and told that they believed she was spending too much time with the petitioner. Cmdr. Wick testified that she then told petitioner that he could not come to her

[2] Dr. Carpenter's diagnosis varied slightly in that he characterized Petitioner's psy-   chosis as schizophrenia.

office without calling first. When this proved unsuccessful, she spoke to petitioner a second time following a fire drill and told him the same thing. The result was that the pharmacy began to receive repeated hang up calls on a daily basis. When Cmdr. Wick answered the phone, however, the petitioner would identify himself as the caller. Cmdr. Wick testified that she reported these problems and then began to avoid petitioner completely. These efforts were mostly successful.

In September of 1995, however, Cmdr. Wick testified that she filed an incident report because petitioner had disobeyed a directive that he not deliver a package to her. An investigation followed and petitioner was given three restrictions: petitioner was not to go in the general vicinity of the building in which Jeanette Wick worked; petitioner must limit his contact with Jeanette Wick solely to business and there could be no social relationship; and whenever he planned to use his grounds privileges he must first speak to some member of the treatment team and indicate what he was going to do and where he was going to be.

In response to a question regarding whether she has had contact with the petitioner in the wake of the incident report and the subsequent investigation, Cmdr. Wick testified that she encounters the petitioner on the third Monday of each month because of her attendance at a committee meeting in the acute care hospital and that petitioner is frequently standing in the lobby when she arrives. Asked to describe the encounter, Cmdr. Wick testified regarding one example occurring in March 1996: "[Petitioner] glares at me. He stares at me. I guess the kids would say, he stares me down." She added: "I went to the elevator, and as I went to the elevator, [petitioner] re-situated himself so he could keep me in his line of vision apparently."

The court credits Cmdr. Wick's testimony. In addition to a demeanor that suggests a high degree of credibility, the petitioner has failed to directly rebut any of her testimony. . . .

The government offered only one expert witness: Dr. Raymond F. Patterson. Dr. Patterson's diagnosis of the petitioner does not vary from that of petitioner's experts or the hospital's diagnosis. He too believes that petitioner's major illnesses, psychotic disorder not otherwise specified and major depression, are in remission. Dr. Patterson, however, does not concur with petitioner's experts that petitioner will not be dangerous to himself or others in the reasonable future if allowed unaccompanied visits with his parents. What is compelling to the Court are Dr. Patterson's reasons for his opinion. As Dr. Patterson testified:

> The last time Mr. Hinckley was in the community, unattended or unsupervised, the risk of dangerousness was extremely high. That was 16 years ago. Therefore, you have to consider past history and what factors went into his having committed that offense, and his subsequent improvement as observed by hospital staff and as reported by himself and by others, and the

psychological testing that demonstrates some improvements in some areas and some concerns that some very core personality issues remain unchanged.

Dr. Patterson also based his opinion on petitioner's recent relationship with Cmdr. Wick. Dr. Patterson stated that petitioner's relationship with Cmdr. Wick bore some "striking similarities to the 'relationship' . . . that he had with Ms. Foster." One of the similarities mentioned by Dr. Patterson is Cmdr. Wick's feeling that she was at times "stalked" by the petitioner. Other similarities described by Dr. Patterson (direct or indirect) include numerous telephone calls by petitioner to Cmdr. Wick; numerous visits to Cmdr. Wick's office and those visits eventually becoming unwelcome; Cmdr. Wick's filing of an incident report when petitioner disobeyed her directive not to deliver a personal package; petitioner's having personal information about Cmdr. Wick and eavesdropping on personal calls; and, audiotapes of love songs petitioner made and gave to Cmdr. Wick.

Dr. Patterson describes the "stalking" parallel as significant because of petitioner's history of stalking individuals including President Carter, President Reagan, and Jodie Foster. Dr. Patterson described such stalking as eventually leading to the petitioner's assassination attempt on President Reagan.

Although Dr. Patterson does not suggest that the relationship with Cmdr. Wick reached delusional proportions, it did raise questions with him regarding whether petitioner became obsessively infatuated with her.

Most important to the court, however, is Dr. Patterson's account of petitioner's past and continued propensity for deception and secretiveness, especially to those responsible for treating him. Dr. Patterson found it significant that petitioner's treatment team had no idea about the relationship between petitioner and Cmdr. Wick until September of 1995, nearly six months after it began. Dr. Patterson found this to be consistent with petitioner's history and the initial failure of several mental health professionals, prior to the shooting of President Reagan, to detect petitioner's psychosis; and the failure of the hospital in the years since his commitment to detect continuing symptoms of petitioner's mental illness. As Dr. Patterson testified:

> There have been in the mid '80's, let's say in '83 to '88, a number of situations where Mr. Hinckley has not told people that are his treaters what he's actually thinking or doing. They relate to collecting pictures of Jodie Foster. They relate to requesting a nude caricature of Jodie Foster. Even up into the day before a hearing on the matter, Mr. Hinckley stating that it had no sexual content, was not nude.

> They relate to his writing Ted Bundy, his writings about Adolf Hitler, Charles Manson. And none of his treaters knew

that from Mr. Hinckley telling them until he was confronted with it by third parties revealing that information to hospital staff.... So, Mr. Hinckley many times has looked on the surface to be doing pretty well, and compared to many of the patients at the Hospital who do have trouble, who may get into fights or may get into disruptive activities, Mr. Hinckley doesn't do that.

Still another instance Dr. Patterson cites of petitioner keeping matters from those treating him include his more recent failure to disclose a possible interview with Barbara Walters (something he discussed with Cmdr. Wick) in which he would be given the opportunity to play his music. Dr. Patterson stated that this is significant because petitioner has told numerous clinicians and others that he no longer has any interest in media exposure.

In addition to these factors, Dr. Patterson also bases his opinion on the results of psychological testing which indicates that the petitioner continues to be "very defensive and represses a lot of his feelings."

FINDINGS OF FACT

Based upon the testimony and documents submitted by the government and counsel for the petitioner, the court makes the following findings of fact:

1. Petitioner's current diagnosis is psychotic disorder not otherwise specified, in remission; major depression, in remission; and, narcissistic personality disorder.

2. Petitioner has a history of deception and a record of screening information he is otherwise obligated to provide to treating and examining clinicians. Counsel for the petitioner has stipulated to everything that occurred during the 1980's with regard to the petitioner. Most recently Mr. Hinckley failed to disclose a relationship he was pursuing with Cmdr. Jeanette Wick or to advise his treatment team that he was considering an opportunity to appear on the Barbara Walters show to give an interview and a musical performance.

3. As recently as March 1995–March 1996, petitioner has engaged in conduct with the chief pharmacist at the hospital that has disturbing parallels to the conduct leading up to the shooting of President Reagan including the stalking of President Carter and Jodie Foster. These parallels include continued pursuit of a personal relationship with Cmdr. Wick even after it became clear that she was not interested, making unannounced visits to her office when told not to do so by her, making numerous telephone calls and, on some occasions, identifying himself only when Cmdr. Wick answered the phone, gathering information about her after-hours personal schedule, recording love songs for her and using the pet name of her daughter in one of the songs, and staring at her in a menacing fashion more than eight months after he was told to avoid her

by hospital staff. The Court finds such parallels to be significant to the petitioner's current mental condition and his pending request.

4.   The psychological testing results indicate that petitioner has made progress but continues to be "very defensive and represses a lot of his feelings."

CONCLUSIONS OF LAW

Request for Twelve–Hour-per-Month Unsupervised Visits

The court credits Dr. Patterson's testimony over the testimony of petitioner's experts with regard to the ultimate opinion of whether petitioner would present a danger to himself or others should his request for conditional release be granted. In so concluding, the court notes that Dr. Patterson's conclusions and the approach he takes emphasize the concerns most important to the court: that is, petitioner's history of deception and propensity to withhold information from those treating him. Although petitioner's experts and his counsel emphasize the progress petitioner has made, especially in the 1990's, the court does not view such an assessment in a vacuum. His current status must be measured against the entire history of this case.

The history of this case suggests a deceptive individual who has, in the past, deceived those treating him in ways too numerous to recount. That history makes it even more incumbent upon the petitioner to be especially forthright and open with his current treatment clinicians. Unfortunately, the evidence suggests that petitioner has behaved otherwise. The court is referring to the relationship with Cmdr. Wick and petitioner's statements to her concerning the possibility of appearing on television with Barbara Walters when he had all but convinced his treatment team that he had foresworn any desire for media attention. Although such transgressions are seemingly trivial, the court does not think so, especially when measured against his past.

Moreover, in considering the opinions of his experts, the court is reminded of a journal entry made by Mr. Hinckley in 1987 in which he wrote:

> I dare say that not one psychiatrist who has analyzed me knows any more about me than the average person on the street who has read about me in the newspapers. Psychiatry is a guessing game and I do my best to keep the fools guessing about me. They will never know the true John Hinckley. Only I fully understand myself.

What is particularly disturbing is that this statement was written at a time when the petitioner had already undergone five years of treatment and had convinced his treatment clinicians that he had recovered sufficiently for conditional release. Statements such as these cause the

court to proceed carefully in weighing current assessments of the petitioner by his experts.

With regard to the testimony by petitioner's experts that petitioner's mental disease is such that any symptomatic recurrence of his
psychosis would evolve over a longer period of time than the 12 hours of
a monthly visit, the court is not convinced. One of the petitioner's
experts, Dr. Heilbrun, gave examples of what to look for as indications
that petitioner is "decompensating," including withdrawing from social
groups and relationships, not attending therapy, attempting contact with
Jodie Foster or the media, and thoughts of suicide. While such apparent
indications would certainly raise a red flag to treatment team members,
the reality of petitioner's history has been very different. The court is
not convinced that the indicators listed by Dr. Heilbrun are in any way
exhaustive, and, given both the ability and the propensity of the petitioner to deceive his treatment providers, the court can easily envision
instances where petitioner is able to withhold important information
that could indicate a relapse. The so-called "Wick Incident" comes
immediately to mind. . . .

Based upon all of the evidence presented and the history of this case,
the court concludes that the petitioner has failed to meet his burden that
he will not be a danger to himself or others should he be permitted
monthly 12–hour unescorted visits with his parents off hospital grounds.
The severity of the petitioner's criminal conduct, and his conduct at the
hospital since his admission in 1982, as well as his current behavior, all
militate against the conditional release he seeks.

Request to Vacate the Stipulated Order Dated April 24, 1987[3]

The petitioner requests that a stipulated order between the hospital
and the government be vacated because, as a practical matter, it acts to
prevent petitioner from being taken on supervised excursions into the
community. Such privileges are referred to as "B–City" privileges. The
reason for this, petitioner argues, is that the order requires that notice
be given to the court and the United States Attorney's Office two weeks
in advance, but that the hospital does not even plan such community
excursions that far in advance.

The petitioner's request is denied. As an initial matter it appears
that petitioner's request is moot. Apparently, the hospital has not
extended "B–City" privileges to the petitioner, so the notice requirement
is not even an issue at this stage. Even if this were not the case,
however, the court would not vacate its order. The court wishes to be
apprised of any attempts to bring the petitioner into the community and

---

[3] That Order provides:

It is hereby stipulated, subject to approval of the court that should St. Elizabeths Hospital propose that defendant be
released from the grounds of St. Elizabeths Hospital accompanied by hospital
personnel, the hospital shall provide two
weeks written notice to this court, to the
United States Attorney for the District of
Columbia, and to counsel for defendant.

the terms of any such proposal (number of staff on hand, nature of excursion, size of group). The court is surprised to hear that the hospital cannot plan such trips more than two weeks in advance and has been presented no evidence to this effect. In fact, given the nature of this case, the court would think that two weeks is the minimum amount of time needed to plan any such excursion.

With regard to petitioner's concern that the notice requirement would trigger a public hearing wherein it would become known by members of the public and media the proposed location of the excursion, the court does not find that this would act as an impediment to petitioner's treatment. If there were such a concern, counsel could seek an order sealing such information at the time of any such hearing.

Accordingly, the court declines to vacate the order dated April 24, 1987.

ORDER

Upon consideration of the petitioner, John W. Hinckley, Jr.'s, Motion for Conditional Release and to Vacate "Stipulated" Oder dated April 24, 1987, the opposition thereto, the evidence presented at the evidentiary hearing in this matter, and the entire record in this case, it is by the court this 19th day of June 1997,

ORDERED that Petitioner's motion is DENIED.[a]

NOTES AND QUESTIONS ON THE LEGAL STATUS OF JOHN W. HINCKLEY, JR.

1. Unsupervised Release. It is an understatement to say that John Hinckley has been kept on a pretty tight leash throughout the period of his commitment. The hospital authorities are obviously reluctant to take chances, and the Justice Department and the District Court scrutinize any decision loosening the hospital's control. Are they being too risk averse? Are they being fair to Hinckley?

His 1997 request was a limited one—an opportunity to visit his parents for one day per month. The Justice Department and the Secret Service would have been notified well in advance of the outings. Would such a short period of freedom under his parents' supervision be likely to present a genuine risk of danger to anyone?

What does Hinckley need to prove to earn his release? Everyone agrees that he is no longer psychotic (even assuming that he was when the offense occurred). Everyone also agrees that he has not committed a dangerous act in 15 years. Has he recovered his "sanity"? Would it ever be possible to say that a person who has behaved dangerously, as

[a] On appeal, Hinckley claimed that Judge Green had improperly ruled that the hospital review board's deliberation process was shielded by privilege. The D.C. Circuit rejected this contention and affirmed Judge Green's ruling. 140 F.3d 277 (D.C.Cir. 1998). [Footnote by eds.]

Hinckley did in 1981, does *not* pose a risk of repetition? How can anyone *prove* that he will *not* be dangerous?

One possible interpretation of Judge Green's opinion is that Hinckley has to prove that he is no longer the person he was in 1981 when he attempted to assassinate President Reagan. Based on the evidence presented at the release hearing, could one conclude that he has "changed"? Should the Court have been prepared to release him into the community without hands-on supervision for one day per month? If so, for longer periods? Under tight conditions requiring frequent reporting for outpatient visits and permitting re-hospitalization upon non-compliance with the prescribed conditions?

Questions of this sort are confounded by the lack of evidence concerning Hinckley's response to conditions outside the highly controlled hospital environment. Although Hinckley had been permitted to reside on the "civil" wards of St. Elizabeth's, he had not had an opportunity for any significant time in the community for 17 years. Essentially, he was seeking an opportunity for a "trial of freedom" to demonstrate his ability to behave properly, and thereby to produce the evidence needed to carry his burden of proof. How should the law balance the acquittee's interest in regaining his freedom and the public's interest in avoiding a premature release?

2. Supervised Release. Based on its usual practice, the hospital authorities viewed Hinckley's request for unsupervised release as premature—he was trying to attain periods of *unsupervised* freedom before he had demonstrated his ability to succeed during periods of *supervised* freedom off the hospital grounds. However, as the preceding notes indicated, the hospital has also been reluctant to allow Hinckley to have any supervised periods of freedom in the community. From this standpoint, it is noteworthy that, soon after Judge Green issued her order denying his request for conditional release, the hospital notified the Court that he would be going on a 6–hour hospital-supervised visit with his family.[a] In light of the evidence introduced at the recent release hearing, the government opposed the proposed family visit, arguing that it was a "conditional release" within the meaning of the D.C. commitment statute and thus required judicial approval. Hinckley argued (and the hospital agreed) that the proposed visit was not a "release" but was rather an "internal matter of patient treatment" and that the court should defer to the hospital's judgment. This argument was bolstered by the practice that had been followed in the past, including the holiday visit that Hinckley had been permitted to take in 1986, and was reinforced by the 1987 stipulation. In a short opinion, Judge Green

[a] Recall that Hinckley had previously gone on a similar visit in 1986 without any judicial intervention, but that the hospital agreed to notify the court and the government of any proposed trips the following year. The only request for such a visit after the stipulation—the request for an Easter visit in 1988—had been withdrawn before a hearing on the matter.

agreed with the government, holding that the proposed supervised release was a conditional release subject to judicial approval. After recounting the recent testimony disputing Hinckley's readiness for unsupervised release, she decided that he was still too dangerous even for supervised release.

Hinckley appealed Judge Green's decision, arguing that the proposed visit was not a "conditional release" within the meaning of the applicable statute and did not require de novo review and approval by the court. For the first time during the entire period of his confinement, Hinckley won. The District of Columbia Court of Appeals ruled that the statutory language "conditionally released under supervision" means "released under supervision of someone other than hospital staff," but does not include trips supervised by hospital staff. Furthermore, the court noted:

> The very existence of the 1987 stipulation—whose sole purpose is to require the hospital to give notice when Hinckley will be off hospital grounds—suggests that the government understood then that the hospital would not otherwise have to give such notice for hospital-accompanied visits. Moreover, after the hospital was criticized in 1986 for allowing Hinckley to leave the grounds for a day with a hospital escort, Congress in 1988 amended the federal insanity defense law specifically to do what the District of Columbia law does not: to provide prospectively for court supervision of all excursions by Federal insanity acquittees off hospital grounds.

> Since October 1, 1996, hospital staff have made 451 trips to D.C. General Hospital with eligible medium and maximum security patients on "B–City" privileges, as well as 56 other community visits to attend wakes, funerals, or special medical appointments at other facilities. In the same period of time [the hospital] has taken minimum and medium security patients on 359 "B–City" privilege trips to museums, theaters, bowling alleys, arboretums, amusement parks, and shopping. Yet the government has not objected to any of these outings nor to the countless "B–City" passes issued before 1996. In response to a query at oral argument about whether the government would in the future seek to invoke court jurisdiction over all "B–City" passes, government counsel answered equivocally that there might be other situations in which the government thought court intervention might be necessary, based on concerns for public safety. But it seems to us that Congress has already struck a balance in the D.C. law between treatment for the criminally insane and the public safety. For the first time, in a case involving perhaps the most notorious patient at the hospital, the government now argues 43 years after [the statute's]

enactment, that a "B–City" pass requires court approval. We do not believe it has made its case.

The District Court's order was vacated in a 2–1 decision, Hinckley v. United States, 163 F.3d 647 (D.C.Cir.1999), and the government's motion for rehearing en banc failed by a 4–6 vote. The government decided not to petition the United States Supreme Court for review, although it considered doing so.

3.   Treatment or Punishment? Studies have shown that NGRI acquittees typically spend as long, if not longer, in a hospital after their commitment as they would have spent in prison had they been criminally convicted. This finding has led some commentators and judges to argue that NGRI commitment is really a disguised form of punishment. Is it possible that the prosecution's opposition to Hinckley's release, even for a few hours—and the court's ratification of this position—is rooted in a punitive judgment rather than a predictive one? If Hinckley were to be released from hospital confinement, even under very tight conditions, would the public feel that he had not "served his time" for the offenses he committed? In Hinckley's case, the problem is accentuated by the widespread public feeling that the insanity defense "misfired" and that he should have been convicted anyway. Is Hinckley "really" being punished? If so, how long should he remain in the hospital?

4.   Civil Liability. In the aftermath of Hinckley's criminal trial, shooting victims Brady, McCarthy, and Delahanty sued him, seeking both compensatory and punitive damages. In 1992, after attempts at settlement failed, Hinckley moved for summary judgment, arguing that insane tortfeasors should not be held civilly liable and that his NGRI verdict precluded the plaintiffs from contesting his insanity in the civil trial. The court refused to overturn a long-standing D.C. rule that a successful insanity defense does not preclude civil liability, even though it may avoid criminal responsibility, and that tortfeasors are liable for *compensatory* damages regardless of their state of mind. Although the court acknowledged that *punitive* damages may not be imposed on a defendant who was "legally insane" at the time of the tort, it nonetheless ruled that the NGRI verdict was not dispositive of the issue in Hinckley's case because of differences between the burdens of proof in the civil and criminal actions: the government was required to prove Hinckley's *sanity* beyond a reasonable doubt in the criminal trial; in defense of a civil suit, Hinckley would be required to prove his *insanity* by a preponderance of the evidence. Thus, because a material issue of fact needed to be resolved at the civil trial, summary judgment in Hinckley's favor would not be appropriate, even on the issue of punitive damages. Delahanty v. Hinckley, 799 F.Supp. 184 (D.D.C.1992).

This ruling prompted renewed settlement negotiations. In February 1995, the parties agreed to an unusual settlement recognizing that the only assets Hinckley would ever have would be future intellectual property rights. The three victims agreed to accept 80 percent of the first $3.6 million paid for the rights to Hinckley's story, as well as revenue from any literary or musical works that he might produce.

Assuming that Hinckley was not criminally responsible for the shootings—and setting aside variations in the burden of proof—is it proper to hold him civilly liable for the same conduct? If Hinckley was "insane" when he attacked the victims, can it be said that he was sufficiently at fault to be required to compensate them for their injuries? Was anyone at fault? What about Dr. Hopper, the psychiatrist who was treating Hinckley in Colorado and was apparently unaware of his patient's stalking behavior and future plans, even in late February, 1981? What about the companies who manufactured and distributed the "Saturday night special" handgun used by Hinckley in his assassination attempt? See Delahanty v. Hinckley, 900 F.2d 368 (D.C.Cir.1990) (per curiam).

A preeminent objective of Hinckley's treatment team at St. Elizabeth's is to "persuade" him to disavow his interest in public notoriety. Indeed, litigation over the past 15 years has shown that any evidence of his continuing preoccupation with being famous is likely to keep him in the hospital. Ironically, though, the victims' only hope of compensation is Hinckley's successful pursuit of fame. How clever is Hinckley? Will he try to persuade his treatment team that his continuing pursuit of fame now serves the interests of his victims?

———